TOOLS FOR TALKING, TOOLS FOR LIVING

A communication guide for preteens to young adults with mild to moderate Asperger's

Julie Hutchins Koch, Ph.D.

A Mee Maw Says Book

DEDICATION

This book is dedicated to Bo-Diddles

(AKA Eli)

Tools for Talking is the first installment of a series of communication help books called Mee Maw Says. You may ask, why is the series called, Mee Maw Says? My step-son Eli calls me "Mee Maw." So, when thinking about what I wanted him to remember about our long talks I thought Mee Maw Says was just perfect.

The most important thing that parents can teach

their children is how to get along without them.

Frank Clark

Julie Hutchins Koch, Ph.D.

CONTENTS

FOREWORD

Eli is my daughter's step-son. When I first met Eli, he had a great deal of difficulty asking for what he wanted, explaining things he didn't understand to anyone, meeting someone new, and not knowing what was appropriate to do in many, many situations. He also didn't make good judgments about whether or not other children at school were truly his friends.

He has come a long way from there. He now functions in the way any child would, with little indication to a stranger that he has been diagnosed with Asperger's. I tell you that, not to brag about my daughter and what she has been able to do with him, but because I believe strongly in the power of education and teaching. Any child, especially a child with Asperger's, is capable of learning just about anything, including matters of the heart. They can learn to overcome the natural struggle with relationships, sharing emotion, and communicating effectively. Young people must simply be taught directly. Your child or student will welcome your help, too; and, it will make you closer. This book describes how Julie has worked with Eli over the years. I believe Eli will tell anyone that it has helped him feel more comfortable and effective in dealing with others.

C. Larry Hutchins, Ph.D.
Educator, author and father

A NOTE TO PARENTS AND TEACHERS ON ASPERGER'S

Julie Hutchins Koch, Ph.D.

A Note to Parents and Teachers

I am "Mee Maw" to my step-son, Eli. I love him very much. He came to live with my husband and me full-time just a few years into our marriage when Eli was just eight years old. It was, not coincidentally, in that same year that we were given a diagnosis of Asperger's Syndrome for him by a psychiatrist. I say "not coincidentally" because it was in that year that the behaviors I had noticed since meeting him when he was five years old became so obvious that I insisted we investigate the possibility that he might have Asperger's syndrome.

I try to be the very best step-mom I can be; but, sometimes I don't know what I'm doing. Of all the things that having an M.A in Human Communication and a Ph.D. in Education have done for me, I never imagined they would be so beneficial in helping to raise my husband's son. In trying to explain how surprising and unnatural it has been to learn how to parent Eli, I must make an irreverent comparison:

Have you ever heard of unusual animal pairings where a dog or a gorilla ends up raising a kitten or an elephant? I have to admit, there have been many times when I have felt like one species raising the baby of another. My step-son and I could not be more different. Where I am loud, he is quiet; where I am bold, he is timid; where I am socially motivated, he is factually motivated; where I am practical, he is theoretical. That has made it very difficult for me to understand him at times. I would give nearly anything to have 10 minutes in his brain to look around and see what I have been missing. The amazing thing is that for as much as I have taught him, he has taught me more. He has taught me about the essence of the human heart: that no matter what the external behaviors, we are all the same inside.

This book is intended to be practical, not scientific, so it will be important to define who will best benefit from this book. The Mayo Clinic defines Asperger's syndrome this way:

Asperger's syndrome is a developmental disorder that affects a person's ability to socialize and communicate effectively with others. Children with Asperger's syndrome typically exhibit social awkwardness and an all-absorbing interest in specific topics.

Doctors group Asperger's syndrome with other conditions that are called autistic spectrum disorders or pervasive developmental disorders. These disorders all involve problems with social skills and communication. Asperger's syndrome is generally thought to be at the milder end of this spectrum.

While there's no "cure" for Asperger's syndrome, if your child has the condition, treatment can help him or her learn how to interact more successfully in social situations (Mayo Foundation for Education and Research, 2011).

There are two important things to remember when looking at this definition. First, because Asperger's syndrome exists at the less "severe" end of the Autism spectrum, this book will have less use to the parent, teacher or caregiver of a child with very acute Autism symptoms. Second, while there is no "cure," Asperger's can be treated by directly teaching a young person how to deal with those social situations that cause trouble for someone with Asperger's.

I have read many books and articles on child development, Autism, Asperger's Syndrome, and personality but few have given me the direct guidance I needed in helping Eli cope in his immediate environment, or that gave me a way to engage Eli in meaningful conversation that empowered him. In other words, I felt like I could love Eli and help him feel accepted at home, but I didn't know how to help him find love and acceptance in the world. I knew that in order for him to be independent and have a full social and spiritual life outside of our home, when he was out on his own, he needed practical skills for talking with others, understanding other's motivations, and a way to independently navigate his world.

Much of my approach with Eli has been based in the traditions of my experience as a teacher and administrator in schools from urban to suburban, elementary to college. It is also, in great part, a testimony to so many wonderful special education teachers that I have worked with throughout my career. Every small suggestion they gave me and each skilled interaction I observed have become part of my Eli "toolkit" and I use them every day.

I have also learned that it is extremely important to remember that people who have Asperger's have the same feelings you and I do, even though it is sometimes hard to tell. So many of the books and articles I read focused on how different Eli and his peers with Asperger's were from others. I wanted to find a way to help him despite his differences, and, perhaps, even help him use the talents he did have, to overcome the communication challenges he had.

Direct instruction can help those with Asperger's identify the feelings of others and know how to respond to them appropriately so others may recognize these feelings. Think of it this way: when a person with a serious visual impairment enters a room, they use special skills, to help orient themselves to the room and to the people in that room. It is no different for those with Asperger's. Unfortunately, children with this condition are often not given the explicit training needed to orient themselves to their surroundings. They must guess at what is happening and what they should do with others. Our society often assumes that children will learn how to function socially by observation. People with Asperger's simply can't glean what is socially appropriate based on what they observe alone. Many young people with Asperger's can learn how to behave in most situations with the proper guidance and practice. We just cannot accept that they will never know how to behave simply because they have Asperger's.

Let me share a moment that really became a turning point for me. Once, when Eli was much younger, he came home from school to find me crying. I had just heard word that my mother was close to death. Not only did Eli have no reaction to my tears, he sat down and began to inform me about some obscure fact about dinosaurs. I went from despair to anger in seconds and yelled at him through my tears. My reaction only confused him.

Later, when I was less angry, I realized I could simply explain to him, in detail, how to respond appropriately to a person when they were crying. I wasn't sure it would work, but I tried. I stepped into my familiar role of teacher and told him that when someone was crying, one might ask what's wrong, ask if they could help, acknowledge that they are crying, and exhibit a range of other sensitive responses.

From then on, Eli consistently knew what to do when he saw me or others cry. I was impressed with his ability to adopt the behaviors I had recommended and the sincerity with which he carried them out. His responsiveness told me that he cared very much for those around him and that he was eager to behave appropriately.

What is important to remember is that when someone with Asperger's walks into a room, it is somewhat like walking into a surprise party. When one has no expectation of what is about to happen, the shock, the noise, and the crowd can be very alarming. It often takes people several minutes to orient themselves when surprised like that. Use a memory of this feeling to understand how frightening and disconcerting it can feel, even in a room with people you know love you. This is how I imagine Eli feels after he comes home from school and enters the house for the first time after a long day away. Who is home? What mood are my family members in? What could have happened while I was gone? Because Eli can't often "read" the room by looking at our faces or looking around the room, he would often have inappropriate reactions to situations.

This book is intended to explain to you how I began the long process of teaching Eli how to learn those things he could not learn on his own. I hope it brings you much help and hope.

Organization of the Book

To make this book as practical as possible, it is divided into sections based on the answers to four basic questions, or what I am calling tools: Who, What, How, and Where. The questions are treated quite directly and can be read independently by your child or with your child. The last question will become the basis for the step-by-step guide, called The Workshop, which will help your young person independently seek out a situation and find answers to resolve it. The book also contains worksheets at the end of each section of the Workshop where he or she can document even more situations and how they were resolved.

Here is an example of how I hope the book could be used once someone is familiar with its contents: if I were interested in receiving advice on how to handle a certain situation, I could go to The Workshop section of the book and, by answering a few simple questions, could find specific advice on how to act and react to that situation. The simple questions begin with the Where, which determines what environment you are in the moment, and end with those that are reviewed in detail earlier in the book: the Who, the What, and the How.

For most young people, the book is best introduced by you prior to having them use it on their own. Familiarize them with its contents and use. Help them decide where to use it and why it is important to use. It is my hope that much of the advice that the book gives is the kind of advice that you would give your own child or student, or perhaps wish you had known to give, but like me, were learning as you went.

Ultimately, parents and teachers will need to model, prompt, and reinforce the desired behaviors. Modeling entails not only modeling the use of the book, but modeling the actual behaviors desired in the situations as they arise. You'll also need to provide the young person with opportunities to reflect on what they learned both verbally and in writing.

Prompting your child or student to accurately diagnose a social situation and use an appropriate response will be important, especially early on, until the behaviors become more automatic. Reinforce the appropriate behaviors consistently with quiet words or signals of support; and, at an appropriate time and place, discuss with your child or student the successes he or she has had, the challenges still to be addressed, and the benefits of using the book.

Because life is complex, this book does not cover every possible situation; so, it is important to familiarize yourself with the strategies in the book and use the Toolkit Worksheets so that they may know how to deal with specific persons or unique situations appropriately.

For the remainder of this section of the book for parents and teachers, I will record some thoughts I have on a few topics that have greatly impacted my understanding of Eli and how I could help him. The topics are:

- abstraction, p. 13
- lying, p. 14
- generalization, p. 16
- rule-following, p. 18
- perseveration, p. 22
- emotional intimacy, p. 24
- ignoring problems, p. 26
- gaming and the use of the internet, p. 29
- Executive Function Disorder, p. 32
- talking to your child about having Asperger's, p. 35
- final words of wisdom, p.39

Each of these topics has forced me to change my paradigm, and ultimately, helped me to approach Eli in a way that worked for him.

Abstraction

You may already know that those with Asperger's can be quite literal. Abstract thought is more difficult and may require a some precision when explaining things. For example, if a child were unwilling to try something new, someone might use an idiom like, "don't be all wet!" "You've got nothing to lose," "don't be a scaredy cat," or "break out." Depending on the skill and experience of the child, he or she might take your response quite literally, actually imagining that you think he is wet, that he has lost something or that he must break something. Therefore, unless it is a very common phrase you know they are familiar with, avoid language that is not concrete. One way to check for abstraction is to ask yourself if you believe a learner of English as a second language could understand the expression.

That being said, feel free to use metaphors of things they do understand to help to explain things that you are trying to teach them about communication. I'll explore this more, later.

Lying

Early on, I found lying to be an issue with Eli. He used to lie frequently about relatively small issues. His lying made me crazy, to say the least, until I figured out *why* he was lying. Understanding a young person's motivation is critical.

Unfortunately, I have found little to no research on lying as it has to do with Asperger's or what to do about it. From what I had learned from reading blogs and talking to other mothers, it can be a problem with some young people with Asperger's.

We should not view lying in a person with Asperger's to be a moral failure. Remember, those struggling with Asperger's are in a constant state of making guesses about social situations all of the time.

Sometimes lying is only a desperate attempt to say what the person with Asperger's thinks will give him or her a desirable resolution. In other words, the person with Asperger's must often make an attempt to "guess" at what is going on around them. They don't know why someone is upset or what someone else's agenda might be simply through observation. This guessing can sometimes result in lying, in my judgment, because interpersonal conflict or confrontation for the person with Asperger's can be so painful that he or she will try to say what he or she thinks you want to hear in order to avoid conflict.

Lying had become a crutch for Eli—mind you, he was not good at it—especially when put into situations where he didn't have the slightest idea what could result from telling the truth. I have learned that teaching him not to lie was not enough. Responding to the child only with the idea that lying is immoral is insufficient direction for those with Asperger's. You must teach him or her how to deal with difficult situations by providing the verbal tools to use.

For example, if Eli is tempted to lie about whether he brushed his teeth or not, I can teach him that rather than lying, or hemming and hawing, or making excuses, he should simply say, "Oh! I forgot! I'll go do that now." I also take him on small "mind walks" to help him imagine what it might be like to be on the receiving end of a lie, avoidance behaviors, or lame excuses. I find that he is especially appreciative of this kind of help. It has helped him want to adopt better approaches.

When it comes to lying, ask yourself "Why is he or she lying?" Rather than a lie, what would you prefer be said or done that would be honest and, at the same time, be productive and satisfying to the other party?

The bottom line is that, in addition to telling the young person that lying is not acceptable, we must also teach the words we wish them to use, in plain terms, when they are confronted with having to explain themselves. Remind them to use those words when you suspect that lying is happening, and praise them for making the better choice.

Generalization

Those with Asperger's can also have difficulty appropriately generalizing the social norms we teach them from one situation to another.

You don't have to have Asperger's Syndrome to know that human interactions are very complicated. Thousands of elements can affect the nature and the outcome of interpersonal situations. So, it is not a huge stretch to imagine that, for someone with Asperger's, social situations can be baffling. Research shows that generalization of social rules can be particularly difficult for these young people.

For example, at one point, Eli had come to believe that if he said "I don't know" when confronted with a question about why he was doing something "bad," he could deflect punishment or consequences. I quickly wised up to what he was doing and told him that saying "I don't know" was not acceptable. I told him he would have to explain himself. This strategy backfired later when my sister told me about his bizarre response to a question she had asked him. She told me that she was asking him a question about some task he was performing (drawing a particular object). In this circumstance, he didn't understand how to do the task but rather than admit that, he become paralyzed. He could not bring himself to say, "I don't know" because of what I had taught him. Instead he resorted to one of a variety of behaviors he had developed to deflect discomfort. These behaviors included what I call the "turtle," where he tries to tuck his head into his neck (like cowering), or the "deer in headlights" look, or the "pose" where he will place his index finger over his lips and look up to the sky).

My sister could not understand why Eli would not just admit that he didn't know what to do and respond to her question with, "I don't know." I came to the realization that he wouldn't tell her "I don't know" because that was the response I told him he could not use with me when he was asked to explain why he was doing something he shouldn't have been. He was generalizing the rule I had made for one circumstance and tried to apply it to a situation where it was not applicable—the behavior came off as odd in that circumstance.

Another example would be that if you teach the child to say, "Hello. How are you?" when greeting a friend or acquaintance, they may not know that it would be inappropriate to say this to a stranger in a dark alley. Conversely, not introducing yourself to fellow co-workers in the cafeteria may seem anti-social to others.

Providing context is everything when trying to help him or her develop viable communication strategies. In introducing this book to your child or student, I make the analogy that working with tools is like working with people. As a result, you will want to talk with them about how tools can be used in many ways for many reasons, and that picking out the best tool and practicing with the tool is very important to using a tool successfully. And, that sometimes, no tool will work.

Rule-following

As Eli matures and the complexity of the human interactions he experiences enlarges, I discover more and more about how he thinks and what I must teach him. This section on rule-following began as a series of interesting observations I made about his behavior in public situations. I noticed that he was resistant to doing anything except what he felt were within the "rules."

Here is one example: Once, after cashing out at our local drugstore,

I realized I wanted a coupon book that was only available at the store's entrance. Having already exited the store we would have to re-enter through the automatic doors marked "in." However, once we acquired the coupons, I realized that we would need to travel back through the store to exit through the "out" doors—there were barriers in the form of metal railings. I did not see the need to walk through the store again. I maneuvered through the railings that kept the "in" doors and the "out" doors separated. I was all the way out of the store when I looked back and realized that Eli was still standing at the entrance, almost frozen, not knowing how to get out. I waved at him through the glass to follow me under the railing but he would not budge. Instead, he walked back into the store all the way around the displays, back through the registers, again, and then through the "out" doors.

When we got back to the car, I inquired about his behavior. At first, he thought I was mad and clammed up. After I explained to him that I really just wanted to understand his thinking so I could help him, he opened up. He couldn't really put into words why he couldn't go under the railing. Guessing at what he was thinking, I suggested to him that he may have been concerned about following the signs placed on the doors of "in" and "out". His silence told me that, indeed, this was his dilemma. I then explained that while following the rules is important, we need to know when we are abiding by a rule that doesn't apply. In other words, I told him, the railings placed by the store were trying to prevent theft and control traffic, so, in this case, it didn't make sense for us to follow the traffic pattern the store had established.

I have used the analogy from the drugstore with Eli to remind him of the barriers he may be building in his mind. I compare them to the metal railings he would not circumvent when trying to exit the store. I have told him that he does not need to wait for a formal introduction to meet someone new, that he does not need a lesson to try something new, nor does he need permission to discover something new. Using examples from real experiences a child has had is a great way to help him or her understand more complex ideas.

While we want to raise our children to follow rules, some of their rigid rule-following could simply be anxiety or shyness about a situation. I've always speculated that the need for following rules in people with Asperger's was due to the difficulty they have in interpreting their surroundings. Anyone can easily become dependent on rules when the complexities of their surroundings are great.

In other words, a significant difficulty people with Asperger's have is often knowing that the "rules" doesn't always help. For example, the summer before his 16th birthday, we decided that Eli might started looking for jobs. When looking for work, no amount of "rules" would help him take the risks necessary to acquire a job. I accompanied him to those early experiences applying for jobs. We would sit in the car outside the business and practice what he could say to introduce himself and ask for an application. We even talked about what he might expect when he entered. Was it the lunch rush at a busy restaurant? Would the general manager even be there? Could a regular employee be of any help to us? Where specifically in the building might we go to speak to someone about applying for the job? What if we were interrupted by a customer when asking for an application? What kinds of questions might we be asked?

The bottom line is that if you notice that someone with Asperger's appears to be reluctant or clingy, it may very well be that they don't know the rules to follow or that they are too unfamiliar with the situation. In these moments, take the time to explain the situation, speaking plainly about some of the unspoken rules about social interactions that are going on. If possible, provide them a little practice in managing the types of interactions they are encountering.

When the child is young, provide him or her opportunities to take chances, do things they have never done before, and sometimes, break a small social norm in order to achieve greatness or meet someone new. Praise him or her for chances taken. Start with simple things like going to the fast-food counter to ask for extra ketchup, or putting him or her on a team with children he or she does not know. Practice taking chances until he or she realizes that social norms are meant to be followed as long as they make sense.

As your young person develops proficiency with the skills in this book, you may want to begin to draw him or her away from the step-by-step procedures found in the "situations" of The Workshop and begin to turn to the Toolkit Worksheets. Just as tourists in a foreign country follow all signs and directions so literally that the natives can immediately spot them as foreigners, you must teach your child or student to use as many clues as possible from the environment to know what behaviors are appropriate—not just those that they know to be rules.

Perseveration

Perseveration and perseverative speech can be defined as :

> ... the uncontrollable repetition of a particular response, such as a word, phrase, or gesture, despite the absence or cessation of a stimulus. Examples in children with autism spectrum disorder include stacking or lining objects up for hours, or becoming fixated on a certain topic, such as trains or baseball statistics (Senate Select Committee on Autism and Related Disorders, 2012).

Perseveration can look quite different from person to person. I have found that with Asperger's rather than general Autism, it is essentially hyper-focusing on something of great interest to the individual, rather than the repetitive use of physical gestures. In other words, Eli obsesses on topics and activities, unlike someone with Autism who might hand-flap or spin. It is important to understand that when I speak of perseveration in Asperger's, it is not just some fanciful phase or idea "du jour;" it is an extended, sometimes lifelong interest, in one thing or idea. I have found that so much brain time and energy is devoted to this subject that they often do not devote time and energy to other everyday topics such as social and practical matters.

For obvious reasons, then, perseveration can be a difficult barrier when helping your child or student acquire knowledge outside of their area of interest. Eli has always been fixated on dinosaurs, dragons, and amphibians (what I call 'all creatures green'). As he has matured, he has become very scientifically minded. He is very well informed about these subjects. Once, when visiting the zoo, it became very clear that he knew more than the guide giving tours in the insect house.

It is important to help those with Asperger's Syndrome understand when hyper-focusing is appropriate and when it may not be. To this day, whenever we are alone as a family and there is a lull in the conversation, and sometimes when there is not, he will generate some random fact about some creature or creation he has made. Sometimes, he does it as a way of trying to fit into the social setting. He doesn't always recognize when it actually comes off as odd, off-topic, and even a disruption.

The good news is that we can use the unique interests people with

Asperger's have to help them understand social and emotional situations. We must only make connections to the topic on which they perseverate—like using a metaphor or analogy.

For example, if the child perseverates on cars, use the analogy that hurt feelings can become scratches and dents on a car; if coins are his or her thing, try suggesting they put coins in their piggy bank of friendship. Even as they get older and they are uncomfortable with you making these literal, and sometimes corny, comparisons, they can continue to act as a readily identifiable cue for both of you. You can say, "Do you remember when you were younger and we used to talk about banking friendship points? When you're on your date tonight and your friend wants to talk about her day, you'll need to bank that time for her."

As you help them draw appropriate connections between the areas of their interest and the social situations they are less secure in dealing with, remember that those with Asperger's have a propensity toward thinking concretely rather than abstractly. As a result, putting some of these abstract social concepts into familiar concrete concepts can be helpful.

Perseveration will likely never cease in a person with Asperger's, but you can use it as a tool to help them learn about parts of their world that they would not voluntarily want to learn about.

Emotional Intimacy

Teaching any child, and sometimes many adults, about the meaning of emotional intimacy can be difficult. All "grown-ups" can remember very confusing feelings during puberty and young adulthood about love, lust, trust, and real friendship.

Imagine what a particularly difficult task someone with Asperger's might have when learning how to identify these emotions and feelings. There are so many complicated cues in human interaction that give us information about whether we can trust someone and whether someone cares about us.

Understanding real intimacy has been and continues to be a real challenge for Eli. Who he perceives to be a good friend at school is not the person many of us would define as a good friend. A good friend to me, at twelve years of age, for example, would be someone who eats lunch with me every day, someone who shares secrets with me, and someone who wants to come hang out at my home with me, or invites me over. For Eli, it was simply someone who sits next to him in class, or someone who doesn't openly reject him at the lunch table or recess (and sometimes even people who openly reject him). Therefore, it is extremely important to teach your child or student very directly what real friendship and love looks like, sounds like and feels like.

This has been so worrisome for me that I have developed a "Relationship Ranking Scale™ " that I hope will be useful in explaining some of the basic terms and questions that your child or student needs to know and ask in order to make a determination about what level of intimacy he or she is experiencing. The Relationship Ranking Scale should be used as a focal point of the book.

Please refer to the section of the book called Who: The Relationship Ranking Scale™ for a complete description of this scale and how to use it. Test the Relationship Ranking Scale on your own relationships to see how it works.

Ignoring Problems

One of the things I have had to learn is how to help Eli stop avoiding problems. I often find that Eli will choose to ignore an issue (and hope that it will just disappear) rather than deal with it. Perhaps this is not unusual for any young person, but with Eli it is a particularly troublesome issue because I can never be sure when he doesn't feel like dealing with or if he literally does not know how to deal with it.

By way of an example, when Eli was about 10 years old, I noticed over a couple of mornings, upon rising, that he would immediately go downstairs to use the bathroom rather than using the one he has upstairs. My suspiciousness got the better of me and I got out of bed one morning to look in his bathroom. I discovered an awful mess. His toilet was clogged and nearly overflowing. Without providing too many details, it was clear that this had been a problem for more than just a couple of days. More interested in his thinking than the mess, I followed him downstairs and asked him why he wasn't using his own bathroom. In typical fashion, he did "the turtle" routine. (By the way, when he does this, his father and I have learned that we have to remain calm, or we won't get anywhere with our questioning.)

I asked him how long he had not been able use his bathroom. After a few shrugs, I discovered that it had been about two weeks. In other words, rather than just report the clogged toilet, his solution was to permanently go downstairs to the bathroom. I cannot speculate (because I still cannot get into his brain) how he imagined it would all get resolved. I cannot guess if it actually occurred to him that his father or I would eventually discover the mess and confront him or if he thought it would disappear miraculously.

This situation marked the beginning of a whole host of ignoring problems that we encountered over the years: ignored homework, ignored messes, ignored feelings, ignored goals. My mother-in-law has argued that some of this might be typical "boy" behavior or just growing pains (my own mother had three girls and is now deceased so it is difficult to gain a point of comparison). However, my husband reports that he would have reported a stopped-up toilet, completed and turned in his homework, among other things, but that he did have to be prodded to complete longer term tasks. He, like Eli, has ADHD (Attention Deficit Hyperactivity Disorder) which, I have concluded over the years, has symptoms that can be easily confused with Asperger's Syndrome. I don't have any easy answers about this issue, but I do know that you are not alone. I have also learned that you yourself cannot ignore these behaviors. Address it head on!

Sometimes, I have tried to outwit Eli's behavior by always 'inspecting what I expect.' This is a technique I learned as an educator. Whatever I tell him to do, I must actually check for progress and for completion. I don't do this in military style, but I do let Eli know that I will be questioning him or coming to look in on his progress. It has helped tremendously and has helped to avoid bigger issues that would have arisen had I enabled him to continue to ignore an issue. The bottom line is to inspect what you expect, not for your own satisfaction, but for his or her long-term development.

As you and your child or student get accustomed to the 'inspect what you expect' idea, it may be helpful to point out that in many aspects of life there are 'inspectors,' such as teachers, bosses, supervisors, and policepersons who may be 'checking' up on all of us.

Gaming and the Use of the Internet

In our household, gaming and internet use has been a big issue. I did not grow up in an era when such computer-based activities were possible. As a result, I was fully unprepared as a parent about how important these things would be to my son. Now, admittedly, many parents, even those not parenting kids with Asperger's may have encountered over use of gaming; however, I noticed that Eli could literally not pull himself away from games or from television. It could literally freeze him in place for hours on end.

In my frustration, I researched the matter with an eye on Asperger's. I will first share a quote with you for which, sadly, I cannot find the original source. The quote came from a website of a now defunct Asperger's boarding school called the Talisman Academy.

> ... [Children with Asperger's] can sometimes become dependent on these [internet] sites, using them as a substitute for human contact rather than learning the social skills that will improve their quality of life. Because individuals with Asperger's and other autism spectrum disorders can be inflexible and tend toward obsession, internet addiction can become a serious concern. There is also the frightening possibility of cyberbullying, as well as the many well-known safety threats in the online world.

This quote helped me to understand why the internet and gaming could be so addictive to Eli. It also helped me understand how important it is for me to intervene. "We fail [our children] when we expect them to control their impulses and avoid risk behaviors ..." (OnTheirLevel.org, 2014).

You might also be surprised to know that for all young people the research shows that the brain doesn't develop the following skills until youth are in their **mid-twenties**:

- Mature judgment
- Seeing into the future
- Seeing how behavior can affect future
- Associating cause and effect
- Moral intelligence
- Abstract thinking
- Seeing what is not obvious
- Planning and decision-making
- Rational behavior and decision-making
- Rules of social conduct
- Understanding rules of social conduct (OnTheirLevel.org, 2014)

It can be deceiving to the untrained person when interacting with adolescents who can simulate or act as though they know these skills when, in fact, they are still developing them. They are in a very real way just practicing them during their developmental years. For this reason, it is critical, especially for those youths with Asperger's, that we protect them as we give them opportunities to make choices.

I contend that Eli has always been about 2-4 years behind his peers in social skills development. I have needed to allow him more time to practice. I also needed to take time to monitor his development closely until he was able to make choices that will help him succeed. Perhaps more importantly, the time I allow him to 'game' is time he will not spend learning how to make friends, to initiate a conversation, to ask for what he needs, to enjoy companionship—things that for him will not come automatically. Young people must have time to develop the sophisticated social skills that will greatly help them later in life.

So, what implications does this have for young people with Asperger's? For our family, we had to set strict limits on when, how often, and for how long Eli was on the internet or on a gaming system. In our home, we have three simple rules: work before play; people are more important than things; emotional and physical health is a priority.

(1) <u>Work before play</u>. Before gaming or getting on the internet, did Eli have his homework done? Had he completed any tasks required for extra-curricular activities? I also would not allow game play during a school week.

(2) <u>People are more important than things</u>. If there is a family event, or someone is in need, attending to them is more important than gaming or use of the internet (and, quite frankly, a lot of things like reading, drawing, playing with toys, etc.).

(3) <u>Emotional and physical health is a priority</u>. Finally, I tried, although not always successfully, to teach the idea that our bodies are important. Eli, and I suspect many kids with Asperger's, tend to live in their head so much that they forget about the body and the heart. This last rule was one that I invoke when the gaming and internet use just simply overrun sensibility, such as on holidays or snow days. At those times, I would ask him to move, go outside, or take time to talk and interact with friends and family.

We have also had to set an example for him. Unfortunately, there have been times when his father or I spend hours on the internet or playing an electronic game ourselves. It is not always easy but we had to set an example; but that is the burden of all parents—to put our personal wants and wishes after those of our children.

Executive Function Disorder

Another symptom you may notice with Asperger's is something called Executive Function Disorder (EFD). This disorder will not always appear in all people with Asperger's but, for Eli, it was indeed an issue. Executive function is hard to identify because it can often be confused with symptoms of ADHD (or ADHD without hyperactivity). Here is what it looks like: Eli was simply not able to manage his schoolwork, turn assignments in, track what was due, manage large projects, or perform other basic activities that enabled him to be successful at school. In his personal life, he could not gage when something needed to be done, even if it was painfully obvious to everyone around him, like changing the litter box, clipping his nails, setting and working toward big goals like Boy Scout merit badges, or planning the time to do anything necessary for living or success. Dr. Larry Silver says of Executive Function Disorder:

Around the time of puberty, the frontal part of the cortex of the brain matures, allowing individuals to perform higher-level tasks like those required in executive function. Think of executive function as what the chief executive officer of a company must do...

1. Analyze a task
2. Plan how to address the task
3. Organize the steps needed to carry out the task
4. Develop timelines for completing the task
5. Adjust or shift the steps, if needed, to complete the task
6. Complete the task in a timely way

(Silver, n.d.)

Furthermore, "... [Executive Function Disorder] is significantly more common in children with Asperger Syndrome ... as compared to neurotypical children" (Attwood, 2006).

To some extent, it is Eli's symptoms of Executive Function Disorder (EFD) that worry me most about his future. While other Asperger's symptoms may make it difficult to make friends or have deep relationships, his EFD threatens to ruin his ability to support himself at the most basic level. Sadly, EFD can also mistakenly give people the impression that a person is lazy, unmotivated, stubborn or uncooperative—all of which is untrue (Glickman, 2013).

What I have learned is that if a young person struggles with EFD we must explicitly teach executive processing skills such as how to break down a task into its component parts, and visualization of results, tasks and consequences. When we teach these processing skills it also must be done in a way that encourages self-reflection or meta-cognition. In other words, we cannot tell people with EFD issues what to do, we must use questioning that helps them think through a scenario and predict an outcome on their own.

Take time every day to discuss what tasks need to be accomplished that day, the next day, or the next week. Help him or her sort out what tasks need to done first, second, third, and so on. Focus especially during these conversations about what others might need from them. For example, discuss why a teacher would need a make-up assignment sooner rather than later or how long it might take to prepare for something in order to meet someone else's deadline.

Break down the steps to achieving their goals. I also recommend that you use a calendar, either on paper or electronically that they can use to develop good scheduling habits.

There is much more to this than simple questioning. Please read more in the final section of the Parent Guide called Final Words of Wisdom. It will give you additional strategies for teaching important thinking and planning skills.

Talking to Your Child about Asperger's

As a parent, I was very reluctant to put a label on Eli when he was first diagnosed with the syndrome. Not only are diagnoses sometimes undependable, I know that self-esteem is fragile especially before the age of 12.

I was afraid for any of us, his father, mother, or other family members who knew of his diagnosis to discuss it in front of him. However, at sometime around 12 or 13 years of age, I realized that his peers were beginning to pull away from him. One friend's granddaughter said that she really liked Eli but "the dinosaur thing was getting old." We even found ourselves relieved in the 6th grade when the students at his school no longer had recess. It was painful to watch Eli at recess. We found him most often standing in a corner by himself while his peers played with each other.

Also, his lying had escalated to the point where he was lying as a means to resolve every uncomfortable issue. If he didn't do something he was supposed to do, he lied. If he did something he wasn't supposed to do, he lied. If he lost something, he lied. It got to the point where we were having a crisis almost daily.

Finally, the issues with Executive Function such as planning, anticipating consequences, organizing, etc. were so confounding we knew we would need extra help and would have to deal with it directly.

As a result, we decided we needed to tell him that he had Asperger's syndrome, and what that meant to his daily life—and the rest of his life. I knew at that time that Eli had a good self-image and truly believed nothing was especially wrong with him. I did not want that to change; but I feared it might if we did not arm him with information about his diagnosis.

To be clear, we had had conversations with Eli about his "personality" and "preferences" prior to talking with him about Asperger's. He knew that sometimes he had a little trouble making friends because he was shy or quiet, and we would address those behaviors specifically. When we had him diagnosed initially, he believed he was going to the doctor to discuss his ADHD and his difficulty making friends.

Even once we decided to tell him I wasn't sure how to do it. I wanted us all to explore the possibility that he could be taught much of what he needed to know—and I still do—but then I realized he had a right to know. I want him to be in control of his diagnosis and have the tools and knowledge to tackle issues that we cannot anticipate now.

Based on a trick I've learned about communicating with men, I decided to tell Eli in the car, on a long drive home after a family get-away. My husband and I figured that he would be relaxed and wouldn't feel uncomfortable having to look at us directly in the eye. (Eye contact can be difficult for folks with Asperger's).

In a brilliant maneuver, my husband took the opportunity to bring the topic up with Eli after we had watched the movie Disney/Pixar's movie *Cars 2* on our portable DVD player. One of subplots in *Cars 2* is about Mater, the awkward and socially inappropriate tow truck (yes, not a tow truck driver, but a tow truck caricature). Mater embarrasses his best friend and main character, Lightening McQueen, repeatedly throughout the movie. Mater speaks when the social context says he shouldn't; he is loud when he should be quiet; he does not understand the hidden rules of the fancy society he encounters, a society of which Lightening McQueen is a part. It is a feel-good movie and teaches that it is okay to be different and that your real friends will be your friend whatever happens.

His father explored the context of the movie with Eli by asking his opinion about it and having him explain what he thought the moral was. I then gently reminded Eli of our appointments with the doctor in the preceding year. I told Eli that the doctor felt that Eli likely has a condition called Asperger's Syndrome and that, like Mater, might have trouble making and keeping friends without some practice. We then both explained that folks with Asperger's usually had high intelligence, high vocabularies, and other traits that are gifts; and, that with help, he could use these gifts to develop many of the important skills necessary for interacting with others effectively.

Eli took it quite well. (Perhaps we soft-peddled it too much because by the end of the conversation, Eli said something like, "Wow, it's pretty cool to have Asperger's!"). To some extent, I was relieved that he felt that way because it was so important that he consider his condition no different than any other physical condition.

Everyone has a burden they must bear; we simply must take the extra steps that our burden requires of us to reach our highest potential. Even now, as a high school student, Eli proudly calls himself a "geek" or a "nerd" and believes that he has special gifts that come with having Asperger's.

So, when is the right time to tell your child? The right time is when it is more hurtful than helpful not to know. When that moment is can only be determined by you as a loving and observant parent. Don't allow your own feelings of discomfort make the call. Things that are obvious to you, may not be obvious to your child.

The severity of symptoms can also play a role in determining when the moment is right. If your child's behaviors are causing other children to make fun of him or her, talking about him behind his back, or when the behaviors are getting him or her in trouble at school, at church or in the neighborhood, knowing may be more helpful than not knowing.

In the end, it is a personal choice to be made by a parent; however, I would suggest parents consider telling their child once he or she can read well enough to read the main part of this book independently and has developed an awareness that something is different about him or her. Telling a child earlier than that may create feelings of frustration or inferiority; he or she may have difficulty accessing additional information about the disorder and/or may be incredulous.

Final Words of Wisdom

Whatever the progress with your child or student is thus far, it is important to have hope, be persistent, and maintain a vision of the legacy you hope to leave them before they leave home and no longer have you by their side day by day.

I strongly believe—and it is why I wrote the book for Eli—that "the most important thing that parents can teach their children is how to get along without them" (attributed to Frank A. Clark). So, here are a few last parting words from one parent to another as you attempt to introduce this book to your child and leave them a legacy of your own words of wisdom:

1) Discuss and Practice Complex Social Situations in Advance

If there could be only one strategy I could recommend to you when working with your child it is to talk to him or her about the social environment—every agonizing detail of the environment. Talk to them about what will happen, what has happened, and what could happen. Talk to them about personal behaviors, the behaviors of others, the behaviors of groups, and the behaviors seen in the world.

One popular way in the field of special education to discuss and practice handling complex social situation is something called "Social Stories." "Social Stories" is a strategy developed by Carol Gray in 1991 (see a reference to her website at the end of this section) to improve social skills in people with autism spectrum disorders, like Asperger's. Don't be fooled by the name "social stories." They are not literature or books read to children; they are tactical cues and descriptions used to educate children when they encounter social situations, whether the situation is in a formal or informal setting at home in school, at work, in church, at home, etc. It is a widely recognized technique used by special educators everywhere; and, is why I want to mention it. However, for the purpose of this practical guide, and to avoid confusion, I will call them social "strategies."

The idea behind a social strategy is to provide people with background information and specific strategies to help them anticipate what might happen in a given situation. They help people who may otherwise have little or no experience with a situation to make appropriate choices when they are on their own.

I have adapted the ideas of Maureen O'Hara (2012) and her interpretation of Social Stories™ (again, what I'm calling strategies) into four simple strategies:

Ask Questions: We don't realize it, but we are constantly analyzing the answers to some basic questions when we're in social situations: who, what, when, where (these are the "tools" of this book). Helping your young person practice answering these questions out loud on a regular basis will help your young person develop skills in analyzing a situation that he or she may otherwise overlook or not recognize. You can help your child answer these questions by simply asking the questions out loud when situations arise that may require additional insight. Early in the process, you may answer the questions for them (although still point out that you are asking and answering a question); as they progress, you might press them for the answers. Whatever you do, try to make the process pleasant rather than punitive. You will likely have to "sell" the idea to your child that this is important. For Eli, knowing the thoughts and feelings of others has not always been desirable.

Develop Signals: Keeping track of what to do in complex social situations can be difficult. You can help your child remember what to do by using verbal signals that harken back to the feelings and actions taken in previous situations he or she has encountered.

For example, when Eli impulsively pulled the pigtail of a classmate in the 4th grade (it sounds somewhat folksy, but yes, he really did), I asked him how that might have felt to the young girl. I asked, "how would you feel if you were paying attention to your teacher and I pulled your hair?" Because I have a mothering relationship with Eli, I even tugged the back of his hair (gently). Give your child a chance to respond and reflect. Harken back to that scenario whenever a similar situation arises again. It can actually act as a "signal flare". I might say later, "Eli, remember the pigtails?" He will be able to immediately recall the thoughts and feelings associated with a familiar incident so that he can apply them to another situation.

Develop How-tos: Sometimes it is important just to tell your child what is appropriate. If I anticipate something might not go well or if something hasn't gone well in a given scenario, I would simply explain to Eli what I expect him to do. For example, when he invited a friend over one day to play games and I later discovered that after six hours of gaming, that he had not offered a drink to his friend (even after I had provided pizza and told them both where they could get cold drinks), I simply had to make a rule about what I (and society) would expect him to do the next time: when guests come to visit, attend to their personal needs. You will see these, again, in the individual scenarios and situations I tackle in the The Workshop section of the book.

Create Value Statements: Similar to how-tos, it is important to help your child develop philosophies or approaches to life that he or she should operate by. Over the years, some of the values I have tried to instill in Eli are: "people are more important than things," or "work before play." They might even look like a question, such as "how would that make you feel?"

Ultimately, these control sentences would be the phrases and questions that your child will take with him or her throughout life. You'll notice that there are value statements in the Pocket Guide found in this book.

2) Provide Regular Preview and Review

Another valuable tool I borrowed over the years from my special education teacher friends is the idea of "visual schedules". Now, I don't mean schedules in the laymen's sense, or even, necessarily a "visual" representation of anything. For the purpose of this practical guide then, I will refer to it as a preview/review.

The idea behind a preview/review is to provide kids with a way to anticipate what will be happening during the day. You may recall that one of the early analogies I provided in this parent guide was the idea that everyday might feel a bit like a "surprise party" to a person with Asperger's. With no outside resources, this person might not be able to anticipate what will be happening from one moment to the next.

By providing children with even just a verbal preview of what they might be able to expect prior to going to any event or activity, they will better be able to act and react. The applications are fairly obvious; provide a preview before going to a doctor's appointment, a new social group, a wedding, or even something less spectacular like placing an order at a fast food restaurant. Providing a preview of what you'll say and do, what others will say and do, and what your child should say and do can be an incredibly helpful learning tool.

Similarly, after the event, I like to add a review of what happened and what we might have learned from the situation that can be applied in the future. A short conversation discussing the successes achieved in a particular situation and adjustments for future situations provide an equally valuable learning experience. As a teacher, I have always argued that one of the best ways to learn is through reflection. So, the lesson here is to reflect with your child often about what worked and what didn't. Use the Toolkit Worksheets throughout The

Workshop for more formal reflection.

3) Don't Forget the Body

With Asperger's, a lot of the research and guidance focuses on behavioral and intellectual interactions. As I look back now on my life, I realize that I have probably met more people that had Asperger's than I realized at the time. One of the give-aways, in retrospect, is how they carried themselves, small hygiene issues, and issues with dress and grooming. Because kids with Asperger's are less in tune, in my experience, with their bodies, they are vulnerable to being picked on. They may not make decisions to care for themselves in ways society expects them to, or they may have small affectations that make others laugh or feel uncomfortable.

While it can be embarrassing for them and for you to talk about the body, take time to explain and coach your child in these seemingly small matters. It is an inescapable truth of life that what is in our hearts and minds may not be acknowledged by others unless they can get past our façade. I would hate to imagine, as Eli goes out on his own, that lack of grooming or strange mannerisms would hold him back from achieving success or having meaningful relationships.

When he was younger, some things could be brushed off by others as a lack of maturity; but, as he got older I found that he did not develop innate interest or insight into what others saw when they looked at him. It might be as simple as wearing clothes that no longer fit, or not taking care of his acne, but it might be his posture or attending to simple issues with clothing accessories. Eli didn't like to look in a mirror, but on occasion I would ask him to go and look and reflect on his image. I would remind him of how handsome he was and that others might not be able to see him the way people who loved him did if he didn't acknowledge what society expected of him.

In addition to this, because of my background in human communication, I was careful to talk to him about how he used his body like standing too close, too far, maintaining eye contact, speaking loudly enough for others to hear, and whatever else might cause others to question his motives or self-esteem.

For example, if you don't reply when someone says hello, they may not assume you are shy; they may assume you are not nice. If you don't have clean hair or clothes, people may assume you are poor or have low self-esteem. If you have strange affectations or responses to everyday things, people may think you're "weird" or deviant.

When Eli was younger, a simple 'song' or 'chant' grew out of our daily body checks: "Have you brushed your teeth? Combed your hair? Put your deodorant on?...etc." We would sing the song together each morning as a means to check in with him about whether he'd attended to his body's needs. Your song doesn't need to sophisticated, but in the end, developing an verbal checklist with your child will help him or her develop good grooming habits.

As parents and caregivers, we cannot forget the impact that our image has on others and ourselves. Work carefully with your child to develop habits and routines that will not prevent others from wanting to know the wonderful person inside or prevent him or her from achieving life-long goals.

My final word on the body is to be sure that your child gets enough sleep. There are many studies that show that all youth still growing (and they can grow into their twenties) should get 8-10 hours of sleep. However, issues with concentration, perseveration, impulsiveness, depression, and obesity are all linked to lack of sleep.

High school is a particularly vulnerable time for these issues (Bronson & Merryman, 2009). I maintained a 9 o'clock bedtime for Eli even throughout high school. I even had to make a rule that he was not to set his alarm any earlier than 6 a.m. (despite a long commute we had to his school each day). This guaranteed him 9 hours of sleep a night. If he had trouble falling asleep we have used melatonin tablets at bedtime to help.

4) Don't Press when Emotions are High

Sometimes the behaviors that Asperger's produces in people can make those around them frustrated and angry. Sometimes we may feel confused about whether the behaviors are part of the disorder, are just teenage impudence and immaturity, or just human. For as much as you feel these emotions, your child with Asperger's will feel them, too. Spending so much time confused about what others are saying and doing can create high anxiety, despair and anger. Failing repeatedly at simple human transactions can cause a young person to lose hope and give up. There will be times when emotions are high between you and your loved one with Asperger's. I have felt a wide range of emotions when working with Eli, some emotions that I am not proud of.

What I can tell you from experience is that if your emotions are high, or your child's emotions are high, there is no point discussing social interactions, previewing or reviewing social situations, or counseling him or her on any matter. Give your child space, time, and comfort before going back to making plans at improving his or her social skills. Work out a signal or a phrase that will communicate to your child that you both need a time out.

When you come together again, reflect with each other about what went wrong. Then, when you feel like you both have some answers, show an increase of love toward him or her, give specific praise, and make reassurances that things will be better.

5) Make the Investment

Keep in mind that each of the suggestions I mention above doesn't require huge investments of time. They simply need be persistent and consistent, small investments each day. On any given day, I might only have a two minute conversation with Eli about a situation or his hygiene or Asperger's. While, from time to time, we may have more extensive, more profound conversations. I believe it is the small daily interactions that have the deeper, more lasting impact.

Remember that part of the "investment" will require re-teaching and fine tuning. Eli became quite adept at some skills over time, but I have seen small, subtle issues arise that needed to be redressed. For example, Eli became very good at greetings. He would greet the family in the morning with a "How did you sleep?" At first, it was quite impressive, especially to strangers and acquaintances, but over time it became redundant. I had to explain to him that part of an overall communication strategy has to be sounding "natural" and that repetition did not sound natural. In fact, I explained that it could sound disingenuous over time. Another example is when he would complement someone but not actually look at the person before or during the compliment. I had to explain to him that this, too, seemed disingenuousness. Regardless of what you teach and re-teach, just remember that human interaction is complex and requires a lot of skill building and practice.

What I realized over time, however, is that making the investment can have a great impact, long after your child grown. My most prized possession is a mother's day card I received from Eli when he was 12 that said that I was "the voice in his head." You will be the voice in your child's head, too. What will that voice say?

6) Have High Expectations!

I hope the voice your child hears in his head will ultimately be the voice of hope and high expectations. One of the most important gifts you can give your child is the belief that Asperger's is not a verdict determining his or her fate. Your child, like Eli, will just require the loving consistency of parents, caregivers, and teachers who always see potential for growth. While folks with Asperger's may take a little longer and require a little more guidance, they can learn the social skills required to be successful in life. Whatever differences remain are okay and are what makes us human and unique.

If your child hasn't learned how to make friends, don't assume he or she won't have them, help them learn how. If your child hasn't learned how to manage money, ask for help, or turn in his homework, he or she just hasn't learned to do it, *yet*.

I hope this book will give you a starting point, a point of continuation or as means of troubleshooting certain areas of development.

References

Attwood, Tony. The Complete Guide to Asperger's Syndrome. London: Jessica Kingsley Publishers, 2006.

Bronson, P. & Merryman, A. (2009). NurtureShock: new thinking about children. Twelve Publisher, New York.

Glickman, B. (2013). Executive Function Disorder in Children with Asperger Syndrome. Retrieved at http://www.aane.org/asperger_resources/articles/education/executive_function_disorder.html

Gray, C. (n.d). What are Social Stories? Retrieved at http://www.thegraycenter.org/social-stories/what-are-social-stories

Mayo Foundation for Education and Research (2011). Retrieved from http://www.mayoclinic.com/health/aspergers-syndrome/DS00551

O'Hara, M. (2010) Using Social Stories to Teach Social Skills: a professional's guide. University of Pittsburgh. Retrieved at http://www.sbbh.pitt.edu/files/Powerpoint%20Presentations%202524%20Spring%202010/USING%20SOCIAL%20STORIES%20TO%20TEACH%20SOCIAL%20SKILLS.pdf

On Their Level.org (2014). Maturation of the Teen Brain: implications for parents, mentors, and society retrieved at http://ontheirlevel.org/whats-happening/maturation-of-the-teen-brain

Senate Select Committee on Autism & Related Disorders (2012). Glossary of Terms, Phrases, Acronyms used in the California Disability Services Systems. California Legislature. Retrieved at http://autism.senate.ca.gov/sites/autism.senate.ca.gov/files/15 20-S.pdf

Silver, L. (n.d.) *Is It Executive Function Disorder (EFD) or ADD/ADHD?* Retrieved at ADDitude online magazine, Retrieved at http://www.additudemag.com/adhd/ article/7051.html

Talisman Academy, (n.d). Retrieved at http://www.autismhangout.com/myhangout/blog.asp?id=401& blogID=92

TOOLS FOR TALKING, TOOLS FOR LIVING

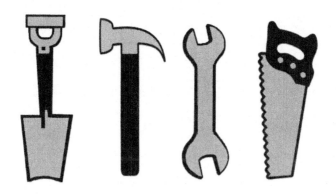

Julie Hutchins Koch, Ph.D.

INTRODUCTION

Getting to know people, getting along with them, and getting them to help you can be hard! Don't worry; lots of adults don't do it well either. This book is made to help you figure out how to deal with people on your own!

My step-son, Eli, sometimes has trouble making new friends or knowing the right thing to say, too. Eli has Asperger's syndrome; so, we have spent a lot of time over the years working on how to help him talk to people. I wrote this book so that he could take a little bit of me with him, wherever he goes. I hope you will read this book as though I wrote it just for you. If you want, you might think of it like your parents or a trusted teacher wrote it for you.

Before I even thought to write this book, Eli and I had a lot of long talks about how to work with people. I asked Eli a lot of questions like: Who did you have trouble speaking with? What kind of trouble did you have? How could you do better next time? Where do you have trouble most of the time? Armed with these answers, we would make a plan for how to handle situations when they happened again. This book is based on the simple questions we would discuss and some of the more complex problems he would encounter.

Now, if you're anything like Eli, dealing with people isn't always your favorite thing to do, but I promise you that as you get better at it, you will enjoy it more! You will make friends and get what you need when it is important. Think of this book as learning to use tools. You will first get to learn a bit about what the tools are used for, then you will get practice using the tool, then you will get an opportunity to use the tool.

What I want you to remember is that learning how to use these tools is really important. People decide if they want to know you, be friends with you, work with you, give you a job, date you, and even marry you based on how you use these tools because the tools represent what you say and do every day!

For example, ask yourself: have I ever worried about:
- being safe or helping others be safe?
- solving a problem in my personal life that involves a friend or loved one?
- being successful at school or work?

• solving a legal or financial problem?

If you have ever asked any of these questions (and I'm very sure you have), you can benefit from this book!

The Four Basic Tools For Talking

We have just discussed why it is important to develop tools for talking with people. I won't spend much more time in this book discussing the WHY, because, if you're reading this book, you probably already have felt why it is so important to learn how to work with people better.

What I want to focus on for our purposes are the tools you'll need to have in order to get better at working with people. I have come up with four basic tools we will use when talking with people. Simply put, the "tools" are the **questions** we need to ask when trying to work with people. The questions (tools) are:

1. WHO?
2. WHAT?
3. HOW?
4. WHERE?

We need to ask who we are talking to, what our purpose is when talking to the person, and <u>how</u> we must approach the person (which can depend largely on <u>where</u> you are). Below are some examples of the types of questions you should ask using each of the main categories:

1. Who am I talking to?

- What is the kind of relationship I have with this person? Do they feel the same way I do about them? (See the next section called The Relationship Ranking Scale™. This section will help you figure out what kind of a relationship you have with someone.).

- What is this person's name? It's important to use a person's name when talking to him or her; it is a sign of respect. However, you may use someone's last name (Mr. Smith), a first name (Andrew), or a nickname (Andy), depending on the situation.

- How much will this person want to help me? How much will they need to know in order to help me?

2. What is the situation or problem?

- What am I being asked to do OR do I want someone else to help me do something?

- What is so important about this situation or problem?

- Is there any additional information I need to know before speaking or working with the person?

3. How should I speak, act, or react?

- Is this a formal or informal situation?

- Should I practice what I say or do beforehand? Do I have to do this right now? Today? In the near future? Never?

- Is there anything I should know about how I'm acting, not just what I'm saying (nonverbal)?

- When is most ideal time to speak, act or react?

4. Where is this situation taking place?

- Is the location appropriate for what I need to do or say?

- How formal should I be?

- Is this something that should be kept private? Why?

The chapters of book will tell you a lot more about the tools of Who, What, How, and Where.

How to Use This Book

This book has four major sections, (1) The Tools for Talking: Who, What, How and Where; (2) The Workshop: Using the Tools in Real Settings (with Toolkit Worksheets); (3) a special section called Falling in Love; and (4) Important Definitions.

The first time you use this book, please read each section before going to the next. The tools in one chapter build on the chapters before it. If you have questions, you may ask a trusted parent or teacher. You will want to talk about things you don't understand and situations that are happening to you.

Once you are familiar with each of the tools, you will practice your skills in the section called The Workshop. There you will learn how to apply the four questions in real-world settings, including:

- Home
- School/College
- Work
- Store/Bank
- Religious Settings
- Legal Settings
- Anywhere/General Settings

Once you have practiced your skills and you have some situations that are unique, you can use the Toolkit Worksheets to develop strategies specially for you.

Now, let's get to work!

WHO?

THE RELATIONSHIP RANKING SCALE™

The first and most important question you must have the answer to when working with people is the answer to the question of Who? Because we must "dig" deep to learn more about who they are to us, the Who tool is like a shovel. You will need to know how much you can trust a person and how close you feel to him or her. Even people that find it easy to manage their relationships don't always know who they can trust and who they can't. Knowing how much you can trust someone is important because it tells you about what kinds of things you can share with them and what you can expect of them. Also, if we are close or familiar with someone, we can use a less formal way of speaking with them. We call this the informal "voice".

I have figured out an easy way for you to figure out what kind of a relationship you have with someone using a few simple questions and a scoring guide. I call it the Relationship Ranking Scale™. It will help you define how well you know someone.

The scale is easy to score and the results will tell you quickly what you need to know about the person you are talking to. Think of the scale like you would talking to your doctor when you are sick. The doctor will ask you questions so that he can figure out how to treat you. The questions in the Relationship Ranking Scale™ do the same thing. When you are finished answering all of the questions, you will have a better idea about how to treat a person. With enough practice, some day you might not need the scale.

To get started, think of a person in your life—any person. Then, answer just five basic questions about that person using the relationship questionnaire. These five basic decisions will help you decide (1) the **purpose** of your relationship, (2) the **knowledge** you and that person have of each other, (3) the amount of **time** you spend with the person, (4) the **living circumstances (proximity)** around the person, and (5) the **trust or good feelings** you have with the person. Each of these decisions will be explained more below. Once you have made your decisions, you will score the answers. The score will tell you if you have a high, medium, low or no relationship with the person. You need to know what kind of a relationship you have with the person in order use The Workshop and to know how to work with the person, including getting them to do something for you.

Remember, how you answer the questions will affect the final score, so answer each question as honestly as possible.

Relationship Ranking Scale™

Questionnaire

Directions: Think of a person important to a situation you need help with. Answer five questions about him or her. Award points based on your answers using the guide for each question. On piece of scratch paper, write down the points you are awarding. When you are finished answering the questions, you will have five scores (or points) for the person. Simply add the points up and you will have a final score.

Important Note: the points you give someone do not reflect the person's value; the points only reflect your relationship to the person. Someone else might award the same person completely different points. So, do not tell people how you've scored them; it may cause hurt feelings or confusion.

Part 1: Purpose

Everyone you know has a role in your life. The people we know in the early years of our life are usually family members. Later, we get to know people we meet at school or in our neighborhoods. Throughout our lives we meet people at school, at stores, at work, in groups and organizations. Each person you meet in life has a purpose in your life. For example, if his or her purpose is to raise us, care for us, or they are related to us his or her purpose is 'family.'

What is the purpose or role this person has in my life? Give him or her a score of zero (0) to six (6). Zero will be a stranger or new acquaintance; A six will be a person who plays a very important role in your life. Use the guide below to decide:

6 points: Parent/Spouse/Child (legal or biological relationships) or the person who raised you

5 points: Brother/Sister/Cousin/Aunt/Uncle/Grandparent (by marriage or biological) or a person you were raised with

4 points: Best Friend/Boyfriend/Girlfriend/Fiánce (this person has to call you the same thing)

3 points: Friend (make sure this person is not just a "1" to you; see "1 point" below)

2 points: A new acquaintance such as a police officer, fireman, lawyer, doctor/medic, counselor/psychologist, teacher or clergy minister or priest who is working with you in his or her professional role

1 point: Colleague/Associate/Acquaintance/Classmate/Neighbor or a person you are doing a business transaction with *where* he or she works (bank teller, mailman, cashier, etc.)

0 points: A Complete Stranger/New Acquaintance (not a "2"); see 2 points above

Part 2: Knowledge

Knowing special and important things about people is a great way to know how close you are with someone. For example, ask yourself: How well do you know this person? Do you know their full name? Do you know where they live? Do you know what his or her favorite things are? Do they know these things about you?

So, what level of knowledge do you and this person have between you? Give him or her a score of zero (0) to six (6). Zero will be someone you know almost nothing about; six will be a person who you know a lot about. Use the guide below to decide:

6 points: We have a high level of knowledge between us. This person knows a lot about me and my family <u>and</u> I know a lot about this person and his or her family. I know his or her full name, birthdate, and favorite things, etc. He or she knows the same information about me.

5 points: We have a high level of knowledge between us. This person knows a lot about me and my family and I know a lot about this person and his or her family. Sometimes I can't remember some details like his or her birthday or favorite things, but it has not been a problem in our relationship.

4 points: We have a medium/moderate level of knowledge between us. We know information about each other like our names, where we live, where we go to school or work, and we know about major things that have happened in our lives. We have met each other's families.

3 points: We have a medium/moderate level of knowledge between us. We know information about each other like our names, where we live, where we go to school or work, and we know about major things that have happened in our lives. We have NOT met each other's families.

2 points: We have a low level of knowledge between us. This person may know information about my life at work or school. We may know what makes each other laugh, but we don't know what makes each other happy or sad.

1 point: We have a very low level of knowledge between us. We may know each other's daily schedule at school or work, but we don't know enough to make each other laugh or to comfort each other when things are bad.

0 points: I don't have any personal knowledge of this person and he or she doesn't know me, including simple things like name, grade, or job.

Part 3: Time

How much time you spend with someone is another important way to determine your closeness with someone. It can't tell us everything about how close you are to someone, but it can give you some additional information. (Don't worry that someone who has an important purpose in your life may not get a high score here. Just score them according to the guide below.) Ask yourself this question: How often do you see this person and how long have you known them? Give him or her a score of zero (0) to six (6). Zero will be someone you rarely see or have just met; six will be a person who you see every day and have known a very long time. Don't worry if someone important doesn't get a high score here.

6 points: I see or talk to this person every day and I have known them most or all of my life.

5 points: I see or talk a lot with this person most days and I have known them all or most of my life.

4 points: I see or talk to this person every day or nearly every day and have known them for more than a year.

3 points: I see or talk to this person about once a week, and have known them for more than one year.

2 points: I see or talk to this person about once a week, but I have known them for less than a year.

1 point: I see or talk at length to this person approximately 6 to 12 times per year

0 points: I see or talk to this person no more than once a year OR I have just met them for the first time.

Part 4: Proximity

Proximity is a fancy word for closeness. For this question, you will decide how close you live to this person and if you are physically close (have shared a hug). How or if you live with someone can tell you a lot about how close you are to someone, but it can be deceiving so we use this score in combination with the other scores. As you answer these questions, be careful.

Ask yourself this question: How much space do you share with this person? Give the person a score of zero (0) to six (6). Zero will be someone you do not share any space with and do not touch; six will be a person you live with and share hugs with or touch, such as pat on the back. Use the guide below to help you:

6 points: I live with this person all or most of the time and we share hugs all the time. If you have to split time between your parents, both parents may receive a 6.

5 points: I live with this person all or most of the time. We do hug, but not a lot.

4 points: I have been to this person's home many times, and they have been to mine. We do share hugs occasionally.

3 points: I have been to this person's home several times, and they have been to mine. We do not hug each other.

2 points: I have been to their home once; or they have been to my home once. We have never hugged or only hugged once.

1 point: I have never been to this person's home and they have never been to mine. We usually shake hands, and may have touched each other on the shoulder or back.

0 points: I have not shared any space with this person (this includes people you may consider friends, but only speak to online). We have never hugged or touched.

Part 5: Trust and Good Feelings

How someone makes you feel is really important. Ask yourself this question: How does this person make you feel? Give him or her a score of zero (0) to six (6). Zero will be someone you do not feel good around; six will be a person who makes you feel really good about yourself. Use the guide below to help you:

6 points: I feel GREAT around this person. I love him or her and I know I am loved back wholeheartedly. I care so much about this person. We share everything about each other. We have no secrets from each other.

5 points: I feel really GOOD around this person. I feel safe and I have NEVER felt uncomfortable around him or her any way. I feel like he or she listens to me, cares about what happens to me and simply wants the best for me at all times.

4 points: I feel pretty good around this person. I feel safe and I have NEVER felt uncomfortable around him or her in any way, even when we disagree. We may struggle sometimes to have a good time together, but I know that he or she wants the best for me.

3 points: Most of the time I feel good around this person. Sometimes he or she makes me sad or mad, but I could count on him or her to help me if I needed it. I would feel just fine having them drive me home, or staying the night at their house if I had to.

2 points: I feel okay around this person. They can sometimes be unpleasant, unfair, or not very much fun, but I would feel okay having them drive me home.

1 point: I <u>don't</u> feel great around this person. They make me feel bad about who I am. I would not choose to spend any time with this person.

0 points: This person makes me feel awful. I feel a little sick thinking about having to spend time with him or her. When I find out there is a chance I might have to see him or her, I try to find ways to avoid it. OR, I just don't have enough knowledge, time or proximity to know how good I feel about him or her.

Now add up your scores from the previous section. And, if necessary, make some deductions.

Special Scoring: Deductions

You should, if it applies, reduce the overall score of a person by subtracting points based on the safety or security you feel with them. You can deduct points on a scale of 1 to 10. Here are some suggested deductions:

-3 points (subtract points from your overall relationship score of this person if): I just don't feel good about myself when I'm with this person, even if people tell me I should trust him or her, or sometimes I avoid this person because he or she can be moody or picks on me.

-5 points (subtract points from your overall relationship score of this person if): sometimes this person can be fun, or sometimes they aren't that much fun. Sometimes I have wondered at times if I should be alone with him or her. Even if this person is a family member, you may deduct points for feeling this way.

-7 points (subtract points from your overall relationship score of this person if): I fear this person may hurt me emotionally or physically. Even if this person is a family member, you may deduct points for being afraid.

-10 points (subtract points from your overall relationship score of this person if): this person has hurt me physically (not just a spanking); even if this person is a family member, you may deduct points for being hurt in this way.

Special Note: Please **do <u>not</u> add** points to a person's score for any reason. The scale is made to protect you from giving too much of your trust to someone or thinking that you can use a less formal voice with someone, when you really shouldn't.

Julie Hutchins Koch, Ph.D.

Relationship Ranking Scale™

Rankings by Score

Add up all of the points that you have given the person and take away any deductions. Then, use the rankings below to tell you what kind of relationship you have with the person. You will use this ranking when you use The Workshop.

25-30 points: High Relationship Ranking

These people are usually a family member you live with or have lived with, a very best friend, a fiancé, a spouse, or perhaps a roommate who is also a friend. There should be a high degree of love, trust and friendship with this person. You should feel good when you are around them even if you disagree about something. You don't really need to worry about what you should say, but you do because you care about them. Use the informal language with these people (see more on formal vs. formal language in the section called Where).

16-24 points: Medium Relationship Ranking

These people are usually friends or family members with whom you may never have lived or haven't lived with for a very long time. However, you probably see them pretty regularly. It may be someone with whom you mostly feel safe and good with like a roommate, or a trusted teacher, doctor or coach. You should feel friendly or close to this person. You should feel good with them most of the time. Sometimes you have to be thoughtful when speaking to them. Use formal and/or informal language with these people, depending on the circumstance. Some people you thought would have a high ranking might fall into this ranking. This may be because there are some things that prevent you from being really close, like not seeing each other very often or, perhaps, they may hurt your feelings sometimes. These people can still be very special to you; you just may need to be careful about what you say and how you say things.

8-15 points: Low Relationship Ranking

These people are usually a classmate, a work colleague, a neighbor, a person with whom you do regular business like a tutor, or the mailman. A person with whom you have a low relationship ranking may exhibit friendly behavior toward you, but don't be confused: you may exchange a regular smile or laugh, but be careful what you say around them. Be polite, but do not reveal too much about yourself or ask them questions that are too personal. Use formal language with these people.

Note: There is a chance that this person could be an abusive family member (someone who hurts you physically or emotionally); if that is the case, consider him or her untrustworthy (see No Emotional Relationship below.

0-7 points: No Emotional Relationship

There are two types of people you may have no emotional closeness with: (a) an actual stranger, or (b) a person who you cannot trust (untrusted).

a) <u>The Stranger</u>. Despite a smile or a "how are you," this person is essentially unknown to you. Even though you may share polite conversation, you must be careful what you say to them and what you share with them. Use formal language with this stranger.

b) <u>The Untrusted</u>. If you know this person well and see him or her a lot, he or she scored in this category because the relationship may actually be harmful to you. You should be careful about how much time you spend with him or her. You may use the informal language with this person if he or she is not an actual stranger, but be careful not to share personal information with him or her.

Practice

Practice with a parent or teacher. Name 5 people you know. Answer the questions in the Relationship Ranking Scale and figure out what kind of a relationship you have with them.

Again, this is important: the points you give someone do not reflect the person's value to you; the points only reflect your relationship to the person. Someone else might award the same person completely different points. For this reason, do not reveal your score of any person with him or her. Use the chart to help you practice:

Relationship Ranking Record

Name of Person	Score	Relationship Ranking

Julie Hutchins Koch, Ph.D.

WHAT?

Do you want to hear some good news about your Asperger's challenge? You can learn how to improve your social skills the same way you learn to scientifically study something! Our second most important tool for learning how to work with people is to know the answer to the question of What. What is the problem? What do we need? What can I do? We must "hit the nail on the head," like a hammer, in order to understand what we need to do when working with people. We must know exactly what we want out of the situation.

In order discover the "what," we must be very sure what we want out of the situation. For example, in school, you have learned that you can research and experiment on ideas. Your research and experiments can lead you to opportunities to analyze and reflect on your findings.

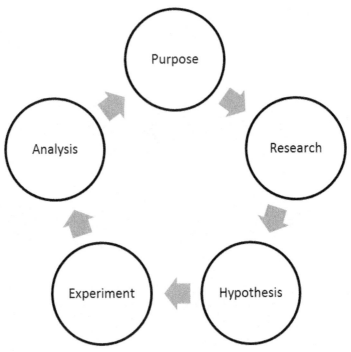

The first step is to find your purpose. If we don't know what we want, we can't begin to research the idea—we can't make an hypothesis or build an experiment and, we certainly can't analyze our results.

I'll bet you're great at conducting experiments in school. In this book, I will challenge you to try this scientific method with your personal life!

Above, you saw a model of the scientific method. All we have to do is to replace scientific purposes with social and emotional purposes.

Below is the same model using the language we might use when working with people.

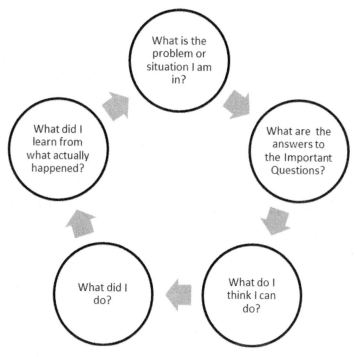

Purpose: What is the problem or need that I have?

Research: What are the answers to the other important questions (who, how, where)?

Hypothesis: What do I think I can do to solve this problem or fill this need that will meet my purpose?

Experiment: What did I do?

Analysis: What did I learn from what actually happened?

In other words, we can apply the scientific method to working with people! So, what is your purpose? Later in the book, when you are using the Workshop, you will be given options for choosing your purpose.

The more you try, the better and more quickly you will arrive at regular results. So, we need to practice. Practice knowing what your purpose is; practice researching the situation; practice attempting new social situations; and practice analyzing or reflecting on our success and challenges.

By the way, you might be interested to know that the more you practice, the more you will realize how your efforts can improve the relationships you have with the people you care about. And, that the better our relationships are with other people, the easier it gets to work with people successfully.

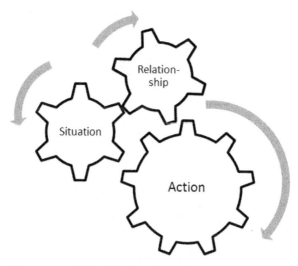

For example, if you work hard to make a friend by using the tools in this book, the more likely it is that your friend will work to be your friend, making tough situations easier to bear. Our relationships affect our actions and our actions affect our relationships. Know that with practice, you can know how to act in most situations and that you can improve your situation by taking action!

Say What You Mean

Sometimes, you may be confused about what others expect of you; maybe you are scared that you might have said or done something that was wrong. In those moments, you may be tempted to say things that aren't what you really mean, or say nothing at all, when something really should be said. You'll feel tempted to do this when you are uneasy about what is happening with the people around you. What you may not know is that saying something is actually the very best thing you can do. For example, if you're confused, ask for help; if you are afraid you did something wrong, explain why you're not sure if what you did was right or wrong. Talking with a trusted adult in your life (someone with a high ranking on the Relationship Ranking Scale™) can really make you feel better.

You will need to learn how to find your purpose even when you're confused. Earlier, I said it was important to "hit" your purpose just right. So, when you don't know what you're supposed to do, here are some tips for what to do when you don't know what to say or do:

Guide for Saying What You Mean

Someone asks...	You feel like saying...	Say this instead...
Why did you do that?	I don't know.	I need some time to think about it.
How are you doing?	I don't know.	I'll be fine. Can we talk about it later?
What's wrong?	Nothing. (When there really is something wrong)	Thanks for asking. I don't feel like talking about it right now.
What are you doing? (when doing something you probably shouldn't be)	Nothing.	Something I shouldn't be. Let me get back to what I should be doing.

Here's one last tip: if you need help or something is really wrong, don't "bury the headline." Burying the headline is an expression that means say the most important thing first. Think of a headline in the news. Publishers put the most important news item on the front page. When you are talking with people, tell them the most important information they need to know first. For example, if you broke a dish in the kitchen, don't tell your mom that you're reading a great book when she asks "what's up?". If you have not completed an important project, be sure this information is the first thing you tell your boss when you meet with her.

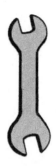

HOW?

The answer to the question *How* is often the first tool we think to use when working with people. Maybe you have been upset when working with people because you don't know how to do something. You may ask questions like: How could I not know that? How can I be friends with these guys? How can I just go up and talk to that person? I hope by reading the previous chapters, Who and What, that you now know there is a lot more we need to know before we can answer the question of How. This chapter is going to give you some really basic strategies for how to work with people, but all of the information about Who, and What and Where will still need to be known. For this reason, the How tool is like a wrench. We must fine-tune and tighten our approach for every situation.

"How-tos" are simple steps you can take for handling a situation that happens a lot. You can make up how-tos for lots of things like how to schedule your day, how to tell someone bad news, how to start a conversation, and how to write a letter. I have made some important how-tos that may help you (1) manage your Asperger's, (2) know what to do in common situations, (3) start a conversation with anybody and get what you need, and (4) how to say what you mean.

1) General How-tos for Managing Your Asperger's:

- Know that **people are more important than things** (including games, facts, schedules, etc.). It may be corny, but in the end, all we have is our friends and family to love us and support us in hard times and in good. Make the investment in people and you will never regret it. Sometimes that means we will have to do things that aren't our favorite things to do in order to show our loved ones how much we care and that we want them around.

- **Be mindful of other people's likes and dislikes**. Remember that not everyone likes what I like; not everyone thinks like I think; not everyone wants to do what I want to do. Sometimes only talking about what we want to talk about or doing what we want to do will make others not want to be with us—this how-to is very connected to "people are more important than things."

- **Make investments in others**. Spend time doing things that other people want to do sometimes, so that they will want to do things that you like to do.

- Know that **your Asperger's is your responsibility**. Asperger's is a health issue and like all health issues, people must make good choices to improve their health. If I had diabetes, I would have to change my diet in order to improve my health. I might get help from professionals to manage my diabetes, but I would still need to actively participate in improving my situation. Asperger's is no different. Get help from trusted adults and professionals, but know that you will need to take some action to help yourself.

- **Learn that work should come before pleasure**. Sometimes, your Asperger's might convince you to spend too much time doing the things you want to do, rather than doing the things you need to do. You will be healthier and happier in the long run if you take time to attend to the things that keep your body, your home, and your work in good order. The small pleasures of indulging in the things you love to do will not help you when your health, your family and relationships, or your school and work are suffering.

- **Conduct regular checks (self-check) of what you are doing.** You can determine a lot about what you should be doing and how you should be acting by looking around you. Ask yourself, "Am I doing what others are doing?" "Should I be?". The answers to these two questions will tell you a lot!

Practice

Can you add any good how-tos to this list? Feel free to add some here:

-

-

-

-

2) Common Reactions

This next section contains how-tos for common things that you should automatically do when you see them happen around you. In other words, "if I see this happen, then I should do this." These are important, because your Asperger's will sometimes get in the way of you being able to see what you should see and do what you should do in order to appear to others that you care about them. (And we know you do!) Below are a few important things I found important in my life.

If this happens...	Then I should...
A person is crying	Ask what's wrong and ask if I can help.
A baby or an animal is crying (or barking/ meowing) or listless	Check for food, water, or seek medical help for them.
Someone is working hard	Ask if I can help or if I should come back later to talk to him or her.
Someone says "hi"	Look them in the eye and say "hi" back (loudly enough so they can hear you)!
Emotions are high—this means someone was recently angry, hurt, had a traumatic event, or has shown you that something is not funny to them	Don't make jokes at this time or later about the topic that caused the emotions; don't change the topic to something informational. Do ask if there is anything you can do. If the Relationship Ranking Scale for this person is medium to high, you can touch this person on the shoulder when you ask.
The conversation is on a certain topic	Stay on that topic, unless you "transition" the conversation appropriately.*

* When you want to switch the topic of a conversation, think of something that connects the topic with the topic you'd like to introduce. Ask yourself

if the topic you want to introduce would be interesting to others at that time.

Practice

Can you think of any other common reactions you have learned? Use the spaces below to add your own!

If this happens...	Then I should...

3) A Basic Communication Strategy

The final how-to that you will learn in this book and use in your everyday life is a basic strategy for talking to other people. The strategy can be used whenever you are having a first contact with someone and you need help or some information. Keep in mind that step 1 and step 5 (both are marked *) are not needed for people with whom you have a high relationship ranking, or at home with people who you have a medium relationship ranking.

1. *Greet the person. Say the person's name, if you know it, or introduce yourself and ask their name.
2. Say what you need and/or ask a question.
3. Say what you will do based on the person's response to you.
4. Thank the person.
5. *Provide the person information about how to contact you later if it is appropriate.

Remember this basic order, especially steps 2-4. They will come in handy all the time! These basic ways of handling the "what" (your, purpose, problem, situation, or need) can be used again and again. Remember the how-tos!

WHERE?

The last tool in our toolkit is the answer to the question of Where?. Knowing where you are will give you the final bit of information you will need in order to know how to work with people. Looking carefully at where you are will help you to look inside of a place, to figure out what kinds of things people do, don't do, want to do, don't want to do, and more. Carefully "cutting through," like a saw, the Where can tell you a lot of information you will need to know to be successful. So, the Where tool is like a saw!

I want to tell you about something called the "hidden curriculum." You may know that, most of the time, when we talk about curriculum, it is what your parents and teachers talk about at parent-teacher conferences, or you may think of it as the textbook your teacher makes you read at night for homework. There is a different kind of curriculum in our world, though, that you can't know by just reading a book. They are the unwritten rules to working with people that we are expected know, but we don't talk about. It is a "hidden" curriculum. We'll call them the hidden rules. And, sometimes, we must cut through a lot of stuff in order to know what (and where) they are.

Here's an example: Some families don't walk around their houses with shoes on—ever! Really, some families and especially those in certain countries or cultures, believe that our shoes are so dirty that we should take them off at the door. If you visit someone's house where this is the rule, it can feel weird. In order to be polite, everyone must take off their shoes, even visitors, even if you have holes in your socks! If you break the house rule, the family may think you are awkward, silly, or even rude. That's an example of a hidden curriculum or a hidden rule. It's just expected that you know it and follow the rule. If you don't you could offend someone.

Think of a situation where you didn't know much about the culture or the environment. Did someone point out a mistake you made or did someone make fun of you? Was there any way for you to know what the rule was before you made the mistake? If not, it was probably a hidden rule. For example, when my son was about eight years old we gave him his first suit. When he tried it on for the first time, he tucked the coat jacket into the pants! No kidding! He didn't know any better, but his father and I couldn't help but laugh. I think he was a little embarrassed, but he learned something about how society expects men to wear their suits.

What's interesting about the hidden rules are that they can change. Probably everyone you know has a cell phone or mobile phone. However, did you know that not so long ago most people didn't have cell phones? It is hard to believe how we lived without them now, but when they started to become popular unspoken rules about what was okay and what was not okay started being made. No one wrote these rules down, people just began to learn what was okay and not okay by watching other people's reactions. As a society, we decided where and how to use them. We decided how loudly we should talk into the phone and about whether or not it was rude to text someone while talking face to face with another person. For a long time, people thought you were strange if you were walking down the street talking to yourself—people didn't know that the other person probably had an earpiece and was really talking on the phone.

What I'm saying may sound like it could become confusing; but, I tell you this because it is important that you know that there are rules (called norms) all around us that we may not know about. It is important that you pay attention to what others are doing and how they are doing it. You can ask questions of trusted people to find out more about what is okay and not okay in new situations. At least now you know that there is a hidden curriculum! Hopefully, the following information in this section will help you learn a lot more about hidden rules in our society.

Formal and Informal Situations

Have your parents ever "shushed" you when someone from work calls on the phone? Have you ever noticed that when your teachers talk to each other, it seems different than when they are talking to you? Have you ever noticed that your parents speak differently to you than they do to their friends? These examples, and many more, are examples of how talking to people can change depending on the situation. They are hidden rules or norms.

We have to change the *way* we speak to match the person and the situation. The first thing you should know is that this is a good thing. Sometimes, we hear from our friends or the media that we should be who we are no matter what—and that's true—however, being who we are is different than being respectful to those around us. The less familiar we are with someone, the more formal the situation will be; the more formal the situation, the more careful we need to be about what we say, how we say it, and how we act. Why? Because misunderstandings can happen when two people who are unfamiliar with each other interact.

Here are some other examples: if a classmate from school says a bad word in front of his teacher, he would get in trouble, right? If he said the same word in front of his friends at lunch, would he be in trouble? Maybe not. Why do you think that is? Because saying a bad word in front of your teacher makes your teacher think that your classmate doesn't care what he says in front of her. It seems disrespectful. However, a bad word said in front of friends at lunch might be seen as funny or cool to the other students at the table. We can say, then, that the situation with your teacher is more formal than the situation with your friends. The situation changes the kinds of words you can use and how you can say them.

Here's another example, let's say that you go into your local public library. Just before you enter, you may be laughing and talking to your friends. Why do people lower their volume, or even stop speaking once they walk in to the library? Because they know that others are studying or reading in the library. They know that others may lose concentration if the people around them are being loud. It is considered disrespectful to disregard other's enjoyment of the library. In a specific setting like a library, the formal way we talk is to be quiet; whereas the way we would talk in a meeting when you would need to be heard by a whole group of people, would be much louder.

So, understanding that *how* we speak depends on *who* we speak to, *where* we are and *what* the situation is are really important to building relationships with others. Knowing which situations are formal and which are informal is critical to your success at school, at work, at home and in love relationships.

When we work with people, we need to know how to speak. We must know whether we can speak formally or informally. It is the first "rule" of safety when working with these tools (questions)! Here is a summary of the use of the formal and informal language:

Description of Formal and Informal Language

Formal	Informal
This is a one way or two way conversation between you and the other person. Neither of you can assume that the other has all of the information needed to understand the message(s) (which includes names, terms, directions, forms, etc.). You should not interrupt someone when using formal language. Do not use incorrect grammar, slang, or bad language. Speak slowly and clearly with as much eye contact as possible. Be careful when telling a joke or sharing your opinion. The other person may not find your humor funny or agree with your opinion. Use formal titles such as Mr., Mrs., Dr., sir, ma'am.	Two or more people can be speaking to each other. Very little background information needs to be said in order to understand the message(s). (That's because you already know a lot about the person). Some interruptions are okay (although don't do this too much). Use of slang terms and incorrect vocabulary are okay. You don't have to look at the other person all of the time. Speaking quickly and some murmuring are okay. Shared jokes and casual vocabulary are common. You may use first names or nick names.
Example One: Interrupting someone to get help	
Excuse me, sir. Would you mind helping me?	Hey, help me with this, would ya?
Example Two: Saying something is right	
That is correct.	Yep.
Example Three: Telling someone you want to know more	
I would be interested in learning more about the program.	I don't know anything about that. Fill me in.
Example Four: Affirmative or Negative	
Yes/No/Maybe or perhaps	Yeah/Nah/Maybe or kind of
Example Five: Comparing	
Such as	Like

Where to Use Formal and Informal Language

Place	Level of Formality	
	High Relationship Ranking**	Lower Relationship Ranking
Home	Informal	Formal
School/University	Informal (classmates and roommates)	Formal (with all teachers, professors and administrators)
Work*	Informal	Formal
Store/Bank	Formal	Formal
Church/Temple or Mosque*	Informal and Formal (depending on the situation)	Formal (and all clergy)
Lawyer's Office/Courtroom	Formal	Formal

* In these environments, even with a high score on the Relationship Ranking Scale, you should take care to speak, out of courtesy and respect.

** See the Relationship Ranking Scale.

Practice

Practice with a parent or teacher. Try to say something both ways. Ask lots of questions about when and how to use language. Use some of your own examples here:

Formal	Informal
Example A	
Example B	
Example C	
Example D	
Example E	

Nonverbal Communication

One of the coolest things about human beings is that we can talk. If you have a family pet, you know that whatever a pet tries to tell us they have to tell us by using sound or movement; they can't use words. What you may not have thought about, though, is that there are messages all around us that people and animals are trying to say. We call these kinds of messages "nonverbal communications." We have to pay attention to them because they are sometimes more important than verbal messages!

For example, when our dog wants to go outside in the morning to go "potty," she will usually start by jumping off the bed. If we don't pay attention to her, she will start to whine. If we still don't pay attention, she will start to bark. She is using nonverbal communication to talk to us. Nonverbal simply means "not spoken". Human beings use nonverbal communication all of the time, too.

Think of a time when you might have used nonverbal communication to tell something to your parents. Have you ever pouted, or screamed or thrown yourself on the floor during a temper tantrum? This is nonverbal communication. Most of the time, throwing a tantrum in this way is frowned upon by your family, right? Indeed, there are certain kinds of nonverbal communication that just don't get us the kind of reaction we want—they are not effective. However, much of the communication between human beings is nonverbal and very effective, as long as we're paying attention. Some scientists say that as much as 60-90% of our messages to other people are done nonverbally. That's pretty amazing!

So, when you are using this book and when you are talking to people you must remember that a lot of what you are saying might not come out the way you want it to if your nonverbal communication isn't right. In other words, we have to get our words right, but we need to get our nonverbal communication right, too. And, while there are lots of ways to communicate nonverbally, I'll tell you about a few basic ways that are important when trying to get the right message out. The four basic nonverbal communication tools we need to know here are: eye contact, gestures and expressions, appearance, and personal space.

Eye Contact

In American culture, eye contact is considered pretty important. People assume a lot of things about you based on your ability to look someone in the eye at the right time. What I want you to remember most is that when you are speaking to someone, look them in the eye. It is part of our society's hidden rules.

There are a few exceptions to the rule or norm or custom, such as when we are ashamed or very sad. For the most part, though, we need to look people in the eye when we talk to them or they may get the wrong "message" from us. Worse, they may think that you are ashamed or very sad when you are not. It is important not to give people that message, if it is not the case. Think about it: if people think that you're ashamed or very sad when you are asking for help, they may become suspicious that they are helping you to do something wrong.

Here is another example: if someone thinks you are acting ashamed or sad when you are asking for something simple, like a packet of ketchup at a restaurant, they may think you are strange or that you don't have confidence. Sadly, we may be treated differently or badly by others if they think we are strange or don't have confidence.

Here are some basic guidelines for making eye contact:

- Focus your attention in one spot, don't look back and forth at each eye. It can make you seem nervous or strange. If it helps, you can just look the bridge of the nose.

- Don't stare too intensely. It can make others feel uncomfortable. Look away from time to time at something that is <u>relevant to the conversation</u>, such as a book, a nearby location, other people in the conversation, etc. Sometimes you can just look down at your feet for a second or two. Don't look away every time you hear a noise or see someone or something else in your view. This can seem rude, like you are not that interested in the conversation. You should be looking at the person about 80-90% of the time.

- Try to relax, enjoy the conversation and truly listen to what the other person is saying. This is the best strategy for keeping natural eye contact.

I have one last note about eye contact, something I found helpful for my son: Look where someone is pointing when someone is trying to show you something. I have noticed that this is an important skill you will use almost every day. It will help minimize confusion and frustration between you and the person you are speaking to.

Practice

You may need to practice making eye contact with others. Start by making eye contact with people that you know love you. You can be confident that they won't reject you and that they will return your eye contact. Once you are comfortable having eye contact during conversations at home with loved ones, try making eye contact with someone whom you have a medium relationship ranking on the Relationship Ranking Scale. You will begin to notice that most people make eye contact everyday with each other and that it is not scary—it is expected. Once you can do this, you can make eye contact with people you do not know well. It will improve the way you are perceived by others and how they treat you—I promise!

Gestures and Expressions

Gestures. Gesture is a fancy word for how we move—how we move our hands, our arms and legs, our bodies. Our body gestures tell people a lot about us, what we're thinking (or not thinking) and how much control we have over ourselves. It is important that people think we have control over ourselves. If they think that we don't, they may think other things about us that we don't want them to. It is a hidden rule.

For example, if I am "fidgety" when I speak to others, such as making lots of unnecessary movements with my hands or shifting my weight from foot to foot frequently, others make think that I am nervous or even untrustworthy. We need to be mindful of the gestures we make so that our words are heard clearly by others and that they are not paying too much attention to our distracting behaviors. In a few paragraphs below, I will give you a list of behaviors and expressions you will want to avoid.

Facial Expressions. Facial expressions are important, too. People expect your facial expressions to match what you are saying. If you are trying to tell someone that you are happy for them but you are not smiling, the person may become confused about what you are really saying. He or she may think that you do not really mean what you are saying. So, the rule here is simple, match your face to your words: smile when you are saying something happy; raise your eyebrows when you are asking a question; furrow your brow when you are sad or concerned. You will need to ask questions of the people you love about what facial expressions are appropriate. You can also watch the people who you believe have successful interactions with others and try to model the behavior.

You will also need to have an honest conversation with a loved one about your gestures and expressions. Ask him or her to evaluate whether your gestures and expressions are appropriate most of the time, and whether there are any areas of trouble you have that may confuse or worry others. Don't be hurt by what you hear. Use the information to help yourself become better.

Gestures and Expressions to Avoid. Please take look at the following list when discussing with a loved one if you are making gestures that are distracting or upsetting to others.

- Rubbing our hands, our fingers or our other body parts against each other.

- Blinking our eyes too frequently or too affectedly (in an exaggerated way).

- Placing fingers in our ears, nose or mouth.

- Snorting or sniffling excessively.

- Making non-verbal sounds that are not related to conversation or natural movement (such as sighing, groaning, muttering, etc.).

- Holding arms or hands above the waist with no intention to express something specific. In other words, normal hand gestures like pointing to something, scratching our heads, clapping, etc. are acceptable when they make sense with our words and expressions. Resting your hands on your hips or folding your arms can be acceptable, unless you are using it to be bossy or reject someone.

- Frequent movement of the mouth that is not intended to produce words.

Practice

Can you list any other gestures or expressions that can be distracting or upsetting to others?

-

-

-

-

Appearance

An area of nonverbal communication that we don't think about as much is physical appearance. Our physical appearance can send messages to others about us that we may not intend. For example, if we wear clothes that do not fit properly, people may think that we are very poor or that we do not care about ourselves. It may seem unfair to you, but how we look does give others a first and lasting impression of us. Others' impressions of us can cause them to treat us in ways we do not intend. We may want a job, but if our appearance isn't appropriate, we may not get the job. We may want to make a friend, but if we haven't groomed ourselves, the potential friend may think that we don't care enough about ourselves—worse, we may smell or appear in a way that could repel others.

So, for the good or for the bad, there are hidden rules and cultural norms about appearance. We must acknowledge that our appearance is important and that we must care for our bodies as much as our minds. Physical appearance can include how we dress, how we groom ourselves and how we hold ourselves (our posture).

Dress. I have identified three kinds of basic dress that you need to know: casual, business attire, and formal wear. Here is a simple description of each. If you are in a special situation that is not listed below, ask someone you trust and who is familiar with the situation to give you guidance.

Julie Hutchins Koch, Ph.D.

Reference Guide to Appropriate Dress by Type

Type of Dress	Male	Female
Casual Worn every day in most circumstances except work. Clothing should be clean, free of holes, and fit well.	T-shirts, polo shirts, or button-down shirts; jeans, slacks or shorts; athletic shoes, boots, or casual shoes	T-shirts or button-down shirts; jeans, slacks, shorts, or skirt; athletic shoes, boots, or casual shoes
Business/Church Attire Worn where you work or other less casual environments. Clothing should be clean, free of holes, and fit well. (Some companies require uniforms, rather than business attire. In that case, follow the company's rules).	Button-down shirts with tie; slacks with belt; laced or slip-on leather or imitation leather shoes (no flip-flops) (Some companies require a blazer, a suit or a uniform. Sometimes uniforms will have polo shirts).	Button-down shirts or blouses; slacks or skirt, or a dress (at the knee or below); 'flats' or heels (no flip flops) (Some companies require women to wear hosiery if they are wearing a skirt).
Formal Wear Worn on special occasions such as weddings or formal dances. Clothing should be clean, free of holes, and fit well.	Full suit with tie or a tuxedo; laced or slip-on leather shoes	Short or long dress (depending on the formality of the event); "flats" or heels (no flip flops); (If you wear a short dress, you may need to shave your legs and/or wear hosiery, as this is the cultural norm).

While some people dress more casually than described above, this is what I recommend. It is better be too well-dressed, than to be underdressed (or dressed inappropriately). However, others will question your judgment and/or may exclude you from activities either way if you don't dress appropriately for the situation, so investigate what others are wearing to certain events and try to dress similarly.

How we dress is very much like the formal and the informal voice—it depends on what the culture says is okay for the situation. While it is difficult to give you a complete set of rules, there is a simple way we can learn what is generally appropriate to wear. Each of the settings (the where) we use in The Workshop has some rules about how we dress, not just how we act. Here is a table that uses the three basic ways we dress in each of the basic places we live and work every day or on special occasions.

Reference Guide to Appropriate Dress by Location and Event

Location	Everyday	Special Occasions*
Home	Casual	Business Attire or Formal
School/University	Casual	Business Attire or Formal
Work	Business Attire	Business Attire or Formal
Store/Bank	Casual (if you are a customer, not an employee)	Business Attire
Church/Temple or Mosque**	Casual or Business Attire	Business Attire, Formal or Special Clothing
Lawyer's Office/Courtroom	Casual or Business Attire	Business Attire

* Special clothing refers to clothing that the religious group expects. Some churches ask for what's called "Sunday dress," meaning a suit and a tie for men and dresses for women. Other religions ask you to wear special things when at services such as a kippot or prayer shawl. Other churches require no special clothing. If you are going for the first time, you will need to ask a member of the religious group what would be appropriate.

**Special occasions might be a wedding, a baptism, a dance, a special party, a graduation ceremony, etc.

Practice

Think of some places you go regularly. Name what kind of dress you should wear there, then make a list of what you should be wearing:

Place I Regularly Go	Kind of Dress Required (casual, business, formal)	What I Should (or Do) Wear

Grooming. Grooming is also very important. Keeping our bodies and hair clean, clipping and cleaning our finger nails and toenails, wearing antiperspirant, combing our hair, shaving, and feminine hygiene are critical to your social and workplace success, and being successful getting help from others. Being aware of your body is the first step.

When you get ready to leave the house each day, do a personal body check. In private, before leaving the house each day and while you are getting ready, you should look in the mirror and inspect your face, teeth, hair, nails, and clothing.

I also want you to do a "smell test." Sniff your armpits, your underwear, and your breath (you can do this by cupping your hand in front of your face and breathing heavily into your hand—then, take a quick whiff). If you smell anything that you wouldn't want to smell from someone else, you'll need to take care of it by washing yourself or using products like antiperspirant, or toothpaste. By the way, don't buy "deodorant." It does not fight odor, as you would think it would. Buy what's called antiperspirant/deodorant products. This will actually stop your perspiration, which controls odor much better.

There are lots of places online that can give you advice on how to care for your body each day but here is a simple routine that I recommend. You can keep this list in your bathroom mirror and check it off in your mind each morning and each evening.

Sample Daily Grooming Routine

Morning
At home: • Brush your teeth • Shower or bathe (be sure you wash your face, underarms and groin well) • Clean out your ears • Comb your hair or style it • Shave (boys, the face; girls, the legs and, sometimes, arms) • Moisturize and protect your face (this may include sunscreen and/or acne products) • Put on clean underwear and socks • Inspect clothing (are they clean, free of holes or tears. Do they fit?) • Conduct a body check in the mirror
Midday
In private, such as a restroom: • Conduct a body check in a mirror • Conduct a smell test of your breath and underarms
Evening
At home: • Brush your teeth, floss • Clip and clean your nails, if necessary • Wash your face • Moisturize and protect your face (this may include acne products)

Practice

Make a copy of the routine above or make a routine that is special just for you, using the form below. You can use the daily routine above to get started.

My Daily Routine

Morning
•   •   •   •   •   •   •   •
Midday
•   •   •   •   •   •   •   •
Evening
•   •   •   •   •   •   •   •

Posture. Our posture is the final piece of our appearance. Slouching and/or strange placement of arms and legs can send the same messages to others that strange gestures and expressions or poor grooming can send: that you don't care about yourself, that you are not confident, or that you are suspicious. Like the other poor habits, poor posture can prevent us from meeting people, getting jobs or getting help. A proper posture is steady and includes a straight back, hands and arms to the side, legs straight, and feet forward. Simple movements are acceptable and natural; just remember to bring yourself back to proper posture often.

Practice

Consider adding posture to your daily grooming routine. During the day you can practice looking at yourself in mirrors or reflective glass to see that you are keeping a good posture throughout the day.

Personal Space

There is one more thing about nonverbal communication that you must know about: proximity (remember that we discussed this in the Relationship Ranking Scale). Proximity is just a big word for how close you stand or sit next to someone when you're talking to them; so, we'll call it personal space. In American culture, there are hidden rules about this.

In Western cultures, like the United States, we require more personal space than other countries:

- About 0 to 20 inches for romantic couples
- About 1 1/2 feet to 3 feet for friends and family
- About 3 feet to 10 feet for classmates and coworkers
- 4 feet or more for strangers

These distances can be much larger when talking to a large group.

Now there are other hidden rules about personal space you should know.

- Don't touch anyone you don't know, unless it is to shake their hand or give a warm hand-shake (this is defined in important definitions at the end of the book).
- Don't ever reach out to touch someone's child or pet unless they are a member of your close family, or you ask for permission to do so.
- If someone leans away from you, they are probably uncomfortable. Do not lean toward them when they do this.
- If someone is walking away from you while speaking to you, they are trying to tell that they need or want to end conversation. Take the hint. Say something like, "*Well, looks like you need to take off. I'll talk to you later.*" Raise your hand as a goodbye signal and walk away.
- At movie theaters and in other group seating situations, people expect you to leave extra seats between you and the

next person, unless there is nowhere else to sit. In elevators, people expect you to stand facing toward the door and as far away as possible.

- In public, don't enter a room or office without knocking first. Knock on the bedroom door of any family member before entering.

Julie Hutchins Koch, Ph.D.

THE WORKSHOP:
USING THE TOOLS IN REAL SETTINGS

So, we've learned what the tools are and how to use them. Now we can practice in real situations! In the directions, we talked about finding the answers to three basic questions when we want to talk with people: Who, What, How, and Where. In this section of the book, you will find specific ways to use your tools by starting with the answer to the question of where.

Here is how to do it, step by step:

(1) **WHERE**: Look for the section of the book that best describes where you are when you are trying to use your Talking Tools.

(2) **WHAT**: Once you are at the proper location (WHERE) determine your purpose (WHAT) for working with that person. The purpose is highlighted in gray. Try to find a purpose that closely matches the problem you need help with. If you can't find your purpose, you can a Toolkit Worksheet.

(3) **WHO**: Once you know the Where and the What, you will want to identify WHO you are talking to, specifically, your Relationship Ranking with that person. If you don't know it, use the Relationship Ranking Scale to rank the person you expect to be talking to.

(4) **HOW**: Read up on what you can say and do (HOW). This is where you can actually read what I would recommend you say. First, I will explain things you should be paying attention to or understand. Then, I will give you a basic strategy. Finally, I will give you some examples. Remember the examples are in gray boxes. The words in *italics* (slanted writing) are the actual words I suggest you say. If it is not in *italics*, they are just additional steps, or actions you should consider.

Generally speaking, with all places and purposes, this is the sequence of steps I use to design your communication strategy with people. I talked about this in the How:

Basic Communication Strategy

1. *Greet the person. Say the person's name, if you know it, or introduce yourself and ask their name.
2. Say your need and/or ask a question.
3. Say what you will do based on the person's response to you.
4. Thank the person again.
5. *Give some contact information, if necessary.

* Keep in mind that steps 1 and 5 are not needed with people who are have a high relationship with you, or at home with people who you have a medium relationship ranking.

Remember this basic order, especially steps 2-4. They will come in handy all the time!

When there is something that does not apply or does not work for your purpose, I have explained why this section is not applicable and have given it a special warning symbol. I have marked the sections that do not apply to your purpose with this symbol:

How to use the Toolkit Worksheets

Use the directions above as a starting point for becoming better at using your tools. If you cannot find a purpose that matches the need or problem that you are having then there are Toolkit Worksheets placed at the end of each section so that you can develop a personal plan for the special situation you are in. I recommend that when you first start using these that you get the help of a parent or teacher (someone whom you have given a high ranking on the Relationship Ranking Scale).

Here is an example of how this works:

(1) If I am at home (WHERE) and I have hurt my mom's feelings (WHAT), I can turn to the Home Section, look for the purpose that matches this situation; there it says "I think I hurt someone's feelings".

(2) Under the WHAT, I will need to decide if the person's whose feelings I hurt (WHO) rank high, medium or low on the Relationship Ranking Scale. Mom probably has a very high score on your Relationship Ranking Scale so you would read the directions for "high relationship ranking."

(3) Read over the advice. Decide if it is going to work.

(4) Practice what you'll actually say by using a Toolkit Worksheet Then, when you're ready, go to your mom and say it.

(5) Afterward, go to the Toolkit Worksheet and write down what you said and how it worked out with him or her.

Practice

Now, get in there! Think of something that you need to say or do and try this out for yourself. Remember, if the problem you are having isn't in here, you can use a Toolkit Worksheet and get help from a trusted adult! Don't forget, if you see a word you don't understand, I probably have put it in the very last section called Important Definitions.

The page numbers for each location are noted here:

There is also a Directory of Situations starting on page 273 for quick reference to common situations.

.

WHERE: HOME

Special note: Because this highly personal setting, we might assume that you know this person a bit better than most. So, you may use informal language unless there is an elder member of the family who prefers a more formal tone or this is a roommate with whom you have a lower relationship ranking. This would also not apply if the person is visiting the home, or hired to work at the home.

Below is the first situation we will encounter in this book. Look for all of the parts of this situation, including the What, the How, and the Who. We are already in the Where (Home).

Remember, if you can't find your situation here, it may be in the Anywhere/General Situations section.

> # WHAT/Purpose
>
> ## Someone has come to visit me in my home.
>
> ## How do I make them feel welcome?

HOW: *Pick the one based on the person's relationship ranking.*

WHO: High Relationship Ranking

Sometimes when we know someone really well, we can be more casual in our words and actions. However, it is still important to be mindful of their feelings and their comfort. Your aim when a loved one is visiting in the home is to offer them food and drink.

1. Start by greeting this person with a hug, a kiss, or a warm handshake (see the definition of a warm handshake in the Important Definitions section).
2. Offer to take their coat or any items they may be carrying. This is intended to make them comfortable.
3. Ask them to have a seat. Be sure to have a clean, comfortable seat available for them before they come.
4. Offer them a beverage and something to eat. Be sure to have something tasty on hand before they come. If you were not aware that anyone would be visiting, a cold glass of water should be sufficient.

Example:

"Michael, It is so good to see you!"

(Offer a warm handshake or hug or kiss)

"Here, let me take your bag."

(Set it down somewhere clean and safe)

"Come on in. Have a seat."

(Show them with a gesture of your arm where a good place would be).

"Can I get you something to drink? Are you hungry?"

WHO: Medium Relationship Ranking

This type of greeting will look a lot like the high relationship ranking except WITHOUT a kiss or a hug; but, a warm handshake should be just fine...or just a handshake will do.

1. Start by greeting this person with a handshake or a warm handshake.
2. Offer to take their coat or any items they may be carrying. This is intended to make them comfortable.
3. Ask them to have a seat. Be sure to have a clean, comfortable seat available for them before they come.

4. Offer them a beverage and something to eat. Be sure to have something tasty on hand before they come. If you were not aware that anyone would be visiting, a cold glass of water with ice would be sufficient.

Example:

"Madison, How are you?"

(Offer a warm handshake or handshake)

"Let me take your coat for you."

(Set it down somewhere clean and safe).

"Come on in. Have a seat"

(Show them with a gesture of your arm where a good place would be).

"Can I get you something to drink? Are you hungry?"

WHO: Low Relationship Ranking

This type of greeting will look a lot like the medium relationship ranking except WITHOUT a kiss or a hug or a warm handshake… just offer handshake. Anything more will make your visitor feel uncomfortable.

1. Start by greeting this person with a handshake.

2. Offer to take their coat or any items they may be carrying. This is intended to make them comfortable.

3. Ask them to have a seat. Be sure to have a clean, comfortable seat available for them before they come.

4. Offer them a beverage (usually someone with a low relationship ranking would not expect something to eat unless you both knew that they would be staying for more than an hour or so). Be sure to have something nice to drink on hand before they come. If you were not aware that anyone would be visiting, a cold glass of water would be sufficient.

Example:

"Mr. Henderson, What a pleasant surprise!"

(Offer a handshake).

"Can I take your coat?

(Set it down somewhere clean and safe).

"Would you like to have a seat?"

(Show them with a gesture of your arm where a good place would be).

"Would you care for anything to drink?"

WHO: No Relationship Ranking

When someone comes to your home that you do not know at all, it is important to know the context of the visit. If you are hosting a meeting or a party in your home when you know that there might be visitors that you will not know and there are others present, you can treat them like you would with a low relationship ranking (see above). If you were not expecting a visitor, and you do not know this person, it is important to know that the scenarios above **do not apply**.

1. Try to glimpse out the door to see who might be asking to enter. If you do not feel safe, do not open the door. You do not need to open your door for anyone you do not wish to let enter.

2. If you feel safe, you may open the door. Deciding whether you feel safe or not is difficult for anyone to know. Sometimes people use clues from other contexts to decide if it is safe to open the door. For example, if it is someone who lives in your neighborhood but you have never personally met, it may be safe. If it is a person dressed in a uniform representing a company and there is a van or other vehicle in front of your home that matches the company name on the person's uniform, it may be safe. If it is a police officer in uniform, it should also be safe. Whenever in doubt, don't answer the door. If you decided that the situation is safe, open the door, so that you may speak to them, but you should choose not to let them walk into the until you know why they are there.

3. Say, "*May I help you?*" This is a common form of greeting with someone who comes to your door regardless of what you think they want. Likely, they are going to offer a service or ask you a question. Do not offer to let them in. You may let them in later if you choose to, but do not let anyone you do not know into your home right away. Stand at the door, bracing one foot behind the door and blocking their view from the rest of your home.

4. After listening to their response, you will need to decide what you want to do. **IF YOU ARE UNDERAGE OR NEED TO LIVE WITH SOMEONE, YOU SHOULD NOT MANAGE THESE SITUATIONS ON YOUR OWN.**

Examples:

If the visitor wants:

to sell you something: You will have to decide if you are interested in buying the product. Even if you are interested, it is still not wise to let them in the house, necessarily. You might consider simply asking for a business card and inquiring later, on your own, about the product from a safe venue, such as the internet or calling the company using a different source such as the phonebook to locate contact information. If you are not interested, simply say, "*I'm not interested. Thank you.*" You may wave, but shut the door and lock it.

you to sign something: People asking you to sign something are usually asking for political reasons or to petition the community for something they want. You will have to decide if you agree with the idea set forth. You will not let this person in your home. These individuals are usually instructed not to enter the homes of those they visit, anyway, and the entire event will usually only take a couple of minutes. If you are not interested, simply say, *"I'm not interested. Thank you."* You may wave, but shut the door and lock it.

to promote a political candidate: Like those asking you to sign something, these individuals are usually instructed not to enter the homes of those they visit, however the interaction may take more than a couple of minutes, if you are interested. Depending on the weather, you may choose to stand outside with this person (or persons) to discuss the matter. If you are not interested, simply say, *"I'm not interested. Thank you."* You may wave, but shut the door and lock it.

to share their religion with you: Like all of those situations above, you will need to decide how much you want to talk with the person. If you are interested, you may speak with the visitors at your door. You may choose to sit or stand outside with them. If you feel safe and that they are really representing the organization/church that they say they are, you may invite them in, but take precautions. Don't let them in unless someone else, a friend a roommate, a loved one is in the home with you. If you are not interested, simply say, *"I'm not interested. Thank you."* You may wave, but shut the door and lock it.

<u>to introduce themselves to you (as a neighbor)</u>: Sometimes people from the nearby homes may want to greet you in a formal way (when you are new or they are new to the neighborhood). Sometimes they'll bring a gift of food or an offer of service. Unless you feel unsafe, it is recommended that you accept the gift of food, even if you do not want it. It is a courteous act (when you accept it, check to see if the dish it is served in will need to be returned). It is not necessary to accept a service such as helping you to unpack or unload a vehicle, but you can thank them and exchange some limited personal information with them. Sharing your name, where you come from, or what you are doing now that you live in the area is polite and usually safe. It is recommended that you chat for a bit in order to establish a positive relationship. Having familiar neighbors is a good investment! If the neighbor says something like, *"Well, I'll let you go,"* or *"Let me get out of your hair,"* thank them for stopping by, wave and shut the door. If you realize that you need to go, say, *"It was wonderful to meet you. I have to go, but maybe we could talk again soon!"* Allow them to say goodbye, wave and shut the door gently.

<u>to complain to you</u>: Sometimes neighbors aren't as friendly or accommodating as we wish and sometimes they may have a real concern about something that you are doing that may be disturbing them. If you are certain that this person is, indeed, a neighbor and you want to answer the door, greet the visitor politely. As with the other visitors, start by saying, *"May I help you?"* Listen to their concerns. If you are able, negotiate a way to resolve the issue. If the

visitor wants to scream, yell, or call you names, end the conversation by saying something like, *"I heard your concerns. Thanks for letting me know."* Wave and shut the door. While it may be tempting to yell back, it is important that you do not antagonize someone who is already angry. It will likely make the situation worse. If you feel unsafe, call the police after you have shut and locked the door.

In an Emergency

Hopefully, you will never have a situation which would require you to let someone into your home for an emergency, but it can happen. Usually, this would look like an official call from a fireman, police officer, EMT (Emergency Medical Technician). This is not the time to offer formal greetings, drinks or creature comforts. Simply direct them to where the emergency is taking place. You will recognize these personnel by their official vehicles, equipment and uniforms. If you are unsure of their identity, you make ask to see a badge. Look for the name or number that identifies this person in case anything goes wrong.

WHAT/Purpose:

I think I hurt someone's feelings.

See General Settings/Anywhere.

WHAT/Purpose:

I've been asked to offer a prayer over dinner.

See Religious Settings.

WHAT/Purpose:

Someone I know is happy but I don't understand why.

See General Settings/Anywhere.

WHAT/Purpose:

Someone I know is unhappy but I don't understand why.

See General Settings/Anywhere.

WHAT/Purpose:

Someone is yelling at me.

See General Settings/Anywhere.

WHAT/Purpose:

I don't understand what is being asked of me.

See General Settings/Anywhere.

Toolkit Worksheet

What are other situations that you have found to be an issue? Name the situation here and determine your plan. Return here later and report what you actually said. (See p. 128 for directions on how to use this worksheet).

WHO: _____**Relationship Ranking**_____

WHAT (purpose):_____

WHERE: _____

    Hidden Rules? If yes, what?_____

_____

HOW (describe below):

What I plan to say (can I use the basic strategy? Y/N):

What I actually said (to be filled in later):

Describe the difference and why (to be filled in later):

WHERE: SCHOOL OR COLLEGE

Special Note: Whether you are in grade school or college, use formal language with instructors, administrators and landlords. Use informal language with classmates, friends and roommates. See Where?: Informal and Formal Situations on page 100.

WHAT/Purpose:

I am worried about a grade I earned.

First, let me say that being concerned about your grade is a good thing! You should be concerned that your grade reflects your hard work and knowledge of a subject. Your teachers, instructors and professors will be impressed that you care about your grade. As an educator myself, I know that many students never speak with their instructors about grades earned. Most instructors will be willing to work with you if you come to them early and often about your progress in the course.

How: *Pick the one based on the person's relationship ranking.*

WHO: High Relationship Ranking

It would be highly unusual if a high relationship ranking could be given to any instructor, administrators and landlords.

WHO: Medium Relationship Ranking

If you have given the instructor a medium relationship ranking, it is probably because you have had them as an instructor in more than one class or a very small class, for a class that has been a year-long, a class that has been very intense such as a laboratory class, or perhaps, you know this teacher well because they sponsor a club you belong to at school. In some instances, the person may know your family. For whatever reason you have a medium relationship with this instructor, it is still important to remember that he or she is not your "friend" in the same way that someone your own age or from your neighborhood would be. The instructor has control over your "fate" (the fate of your grade, your GPA, future college or job applications).

Furthermore, your instructor deserves respectful and mannerly behavior from you. Behaving this way, may also help boost your chances of negotiating your grade.

1. Greet your teacher/instructor/professor. With a medium relationship, you can assume that he or she knows you and your name.
2. State your purpose in visiting with him or her.
3. Ask for what you are hoping can happen to improve your situation.
4. Answer any questions they have honestly and concisely (be brief).
5. Following their response, restate anything that they may have asked you to do, and write it down. Writing it down not only helps you remember what they said, but it will impress them with the fact you are sincere and want to improve things.
6. Thank them very kindly for the help.

Example:

Hi, Dr. Jones, do you have a minute? I wanted to speak with you about my grade on the most recent exam. I was wondering if there is any way that I could pull up this grade or, at least, prevent myself from getting this kind of grade in the future? I am willing to work hard and I'd like to get a good grade in this course.

WHO: Low Relationship Ranking

1. Greet your teacher/instructor/professor. With a low relationship ranking, you should state your name and the course you are referring to.
2. State your purpose for visiting with them.
3. Ask for what you are hoping can happen to improve your situation.
4. Answer any questions they have honestly and concisely (be brief).
5. Following their response, restate anything that they may have asked you to do, and write it down.
6. Thank them very kindly for the help.

Example:

Hi, Mr. Yuan. I'm Eli. I'm in your 2nd hour U.S. History class. Is it possible to speak to you about my grade or do I need to make an appointment? I am really concerned about my mid-term grade. Is there any way I can pull this up now or by the end of the term? I am willing to work hard and I'd like to get a good grade in this course.

WHO: No Relationship Ranking

In grade school, it is unlikely that you would ever have a teacher with whom you have no relationship; but, at the college level, you may be in a class with over 200 students, or you may have only met the lab instructor or teaching assistant and not the actual professor. So, you may be in a situation where you might give someone a "no relationship" ranking.

1. Greet your teacher/instructor/professor. With no relationship, you should identify the course you are referring to.

2. State your name.

3. State your purpose for visiting with him or her.

4. Ask for what you are hoping can happen to improve your situation.

5. Answer any questions they have honestly and concisely (be brief).

6. Following their response, restate anything that they may have asked you to do, and write it down.

7. Thank them very kindly for the help.

Example:

Hi, Dr. Farmer, I am a student in your 2:30 Biology class. My name is Sam Wilson. I wanted to speak with you personally about my final grade. I was getting a C prior to the final exam but I did not do well on it. I wanted you to know that I have been meeting with a tutor all semester and met with your teaching assistant before. I knew this class would be difficult for me but I worked very hard and am devastated by my grade. Is there anything more I can do to change your final assessment of me? Would it be okay to speak with you about this now?

In an Emergency

You should not be concerned about your grade during an emergency. The emergency should be dealt with first. See important definitions regarding what is considered an emergency. Go to Important Definitions.

WHAT/Purpose:

My landlord or dorm advisor is upset with me.

HOW: *Pick the one based on the person's relationship ranking.*

WHO: High Relationship Ranking

It would be highly unusual that a high relationship ranking could be given to any instructor, administrator or landlord. If for some reason you do, use the Medium Relationship ranking.

Who: Medium Relationship Ranking

It is possible that you might have a medium relationship with a landlord or dorm advisor. They may live near you, such as down the hall, and you may see them often, especially with a dorm advisor, whose job it is to help you adjust to college life. Your exact scenario will also depend on where you are when you are approached.

1a. If you are approached in your room or apartment, hopefully you can invite him or her into your room or apartment. This will add an intimacy to the conversation that may help them to approach you more reasonably. Be sure that your place is clean and tidy. Whatever concern he or she might have could be aggravated by the condition of your personal space. Is it messy? Smelly? Dirty? If you can't invite them in because your place is a mess, invite them to sit with you on the front stoop or sit in the dorm lounge.

1b. If you are approached in the lounge or in the office, make the time to speak with him or her, even if it is a little inconvenient for you. Your willingness to meet will help improve the final outcome of the conversation.

2. Use all courtesies prior to starting the conversation. Ask about his or her well-being. Pay a compliment or follow up with a previous conversation. (However, don't do this if the person is angry! It could backfire or make you seem false).

3. Listen to the concerns patiently. Repeat back what you think he or she is telling you. If you are able, negotiate a way to resolve the issue. Be sure you know your rights and responsibilities for living at the property.

4. If the he or she begins to scream, yell, or call you names, end the conversation by saying something like, "I heard your concerns.

Thanks for letting me know. You're obviously upset and this may not be the best time to talk about it. I'll be willing to talk about it when we can talk about this more calmly."

Example:

Hi, Gloria. How are you? How is your family doing? It was so nice to meet them the other day.

(Allow a response).

So, how can I help you?

(Allow a response. Listen patiently to the complaint).

So, you've had some complaints that I have been parking in the wrong place. Is that right? Well, I want to follow the rules and I don't want anyone upset. Can you show me where exactly I am supposed to be parking? Once I'm clear, I will be sure never to make the mistake again.

WHO: Low/No Relationship Ranking

1a. If you are approached in your room or apartment, you don't have to let him or her in your home but you will want them to feel comfortable—again, this can help a person feel more relaxed in the situation, which will hopefully help the outcome.

1b. If you are approached in the lounge or in the office, make the time to speak with him or her, even if it is a little inconvenient for you. Your willingness to meet will help improve the final outcome of the conversation.

2. Use courtesy prior to starting the conversation. Ask how he or she is or ask how you can help. (Again, if they are mad, this might backfire; so don't do this step.)

3. Listen to the concerns patiently. Repeat back what you think they are telling you. If you are able, negotiate a way to resolve the issue. Be sure you know your rights and responsibilities for living at the property.

4. If the he or she begins to scream, yell, or call you names, end the conversation by saying something like, "I heard your concerns. Thanks for letting me know. You're obviously upset and this may not be the best time to talk about it. I'll be willing to talk about it when we can talk about it more calmly."

Example:

Good morning, Mr. Martinez. How are you?

(Allow a response).

So, how can I help you?

(Allow a response. Listen patiently to the complaint).

I'm really sorry that my music has been too loud. I feel terrible. I don't want anyone to be upset. Can I show you my speakers and ask you what setting would be too high? Once I'm clear, I will try not to bother anyone with my music again.

In an Emergency

A complaint from a landlord or dorm advisor in an emergency situation may very well involve the police or other emergency personnel. Accommodate his or her request immediately. No conversation is necessary.

WHAT/Purpose:

A classmate is bullying me.

Special Note: It is not okay for anyone to bully you. You must be careful whom you befriend. Asperger's can sometimes make it difficult for you to know that you are being bullied. Bullies can be confused for friends because they may be part of a group of your friends. If someone in your group of friends likes to make jokes about you or makes you feel bad about yourself, or puts you down, he or she is not really your friend. Use the Relationship Ranking Scale™ to rank this person separately from your other friends to determine if you can trust him or her.

HOW: *Pick the one based on the person's relationship ranking.*

WHO: High Relationship Ranking:

 It would be highly unusual that a high relationship ranking could be given to a bully. While a brother or sister could be bullying you at home or at school, the following medium to low or no relationship rankings descriptions will work equally well.

WHO: Medium/Low Relationship Ranking

One important thing to remember about bullies is that their intention is to make themselves feel better or increase their sense of their own importance or "status." There are a lot of reasons people bully others. Some bullying happens because the school or college has a culture that fosters it, say in very competitive places like athletic clubs and teams. Some bullying happens because the bully has personal, family or social problems that make him or her feel mean or angry toward others. Some bullying happens because the victim may be what researchers call "provocative". This just means that victims can sometimes have behaviors that make it easy for a bully to be cruel. While it is never okay to bully, some victims give silent permission to bullies by behaving in ways that are outside of the normal behaviors for a particular culture or situation. Some victims may behave in ways that remind the bully of his or her own unhappiness, such as pointing out a bully's faults. Other victims react to bullying in a way that makes the bully feel even more powerful or rewards him or her for bullying. Your goal is to prevent the bully from getting what he or she needs to feel better.

Below are some basic strategies. With any of the strategies, remember that when things get bad and you can no longer deal with the bully, you must report the behavior to a school official, whether it be a teacher, principal, professor, dorm advisor, counselor, or a parent.

Laugh with the bully. If the bully makes a joke about you, you can take away his or her power to hurt you in front of others by laughing at the joke with him. While it is not okay for this person to make fun of you, laughing with the bully shows them that you cannot be hurt by words. It also tells the bully's audience (his friends, your classmate's, etc.) that you are not a good "victim," that bullying you will not gain him or her any additional status or power.

Name the behavior. This strategy simply asks the victim to identify in words in front of the bully and anyone listening what the bullying is doing. It is important in this strategy, not to be cruel, just genuine. For example, if a bully has just said something mean to you, simply say, "You are being a bully. You are doing it to make yourself feel better about something that is bothering you. It will not work with me." Once you have named the behavior, walk away.

Avoid the bully. Many victims of bullying continue to put themselves in situations that provide the bully an opportunity to bully. Taking away the opportunity can sometimes be the easiest way to stop it. If the bully is part of a group of friends that you choose to hang out with, then choose not to hang out with the group if the bully is there. Invite the friends that you love and trust to do activities that do not include the bully and where the bully cannot come. If or when the bully arrives at an event, politely excuse yourself or go to another area at the event or another place in the room. You do not need to tell others why you are really leaving. Tell your closest friends with whom you have a high relationship ranking that the bully makes you uncomfortable and that you will not be participating in events that include him or her.

Tell an official. Telling a school official about a bully is probably what you've been told throughout your life is the best first defense against a bully; and, when things are really bad, you really must tell someone official. However, as you get older, you will learn that this strategy will not always work. Bullies often retaliate (may behave worse toward you at a later time) when they discover you have "tattled" on them. Also, some officials have less power than others to really help you, or even with great power (such as the police), cannot act on your reports of bullying the way you would hope they could. Besides, the worst kind of bullies, bully in secret. No one sees the bullying. I recommend that you try one of the first three strategies before telling an official. It is a hard life lesson, but there are no easy solutions for all of life's problems.

WHO: No Relationship or In an Emergency

When you have no relationship with a bully, it could be because he or she is an actual stranger or because he or she has scored a no relationship ranking on the Relationship Ranking Scale , meaning he or she is well known to you but you do not trust him or her. Each of these situations requires a different strategy.

If he or she is NOT an actual stranger, use the strategies for the medium/low relationship above.

If he or she is an actual stranger, get away from this person as quickly as you can and attempt to get to a public or safe place immediately. This would be considered an emergency. A complete stranger who chooses to bully you may very well be mentally ill or have criminal intentions. This is true "stranger danger"!

Toolkit Worksheet

What are other situations that you have found to be an issue? Name the situation here and determine your plan. Return here later and report what you actually said. (See p. 128 for directions on how to use this worksheet).

WHO: _____**Relationship Ranking**_____

WHAT (purpose):_____

WHERE: _____

   Hidden Rules? If yes, what?_____

_____

HOW (describe below):

What I plan to say (can I use the basic strategy? Y/N):

What I actually said (to be filled in later):

Describe the difference and why (to be filled in later):

Julie Hutchins Koch, Ph.D.

WHERE: WORK

Special Note: Use the formal register at work, unless there is high relationship ranking.

WHAT/Purpose:

I don't understand what my boss wants me to do.

One of the things I learned from my father is that if you are given a job by your employer, you need to get the job done without making trouble or difficulty for your boss. In other words, learn everything you can while you are training so that you can take over the job quickly, so that you will not have to disturb your boss with frequent questions or problems, so that your boss will not be sorry he or she hired you to do the work. However, it is important that the job be done correctly. And, whatever you do, don't freeze up when you are confused. Your Asperger's may make you want to freeze, or it may make you want to give up and go do something else you'd rather do. Worse, you may want to ignore the issue. This section will help you develop some strategies.

HOW: *Pick the one based on the person's relationship ranking.*

WHO: High Relationship Ranking

 See Medium/Low Relationship Ranking. In the event that you work for a relative or loved one and have high relationship ranking, you'll still want to be professional on the job. Use the strategies below to find just the right approach.

WHO: Medium/Low Relationship Ranking

Use this simple approach when you are confused or don't know how to do something assigned to you on the job:

1. Educate yourself.

2. Ask someone you know.

3. If all else fails, ask your boss.

Let's break it down:

(1) **Educate** yourself using the materials already given to you. It is likely you have been given or been given access to, most everything you need. The exception is that sometimes we have to do things on the job that are not written into manuals or that are more "political" in nature.

(2) **Ask a familiar and trusted co-worker.** When I say trusted, I mean, someone with whom you have higher relationship ranking (on the Relationship Ranking Scale) than others. If there is no one you trust, then ask the person who is most familiar with the task you are asking about. Take notes, so that you do not have ask the same question again. At that time, you may also want to ask additional questions about the matter that might arise in different situations.

(3) **Ask your boss.** If you must ask your boss, whatever you do, ask any questions of clarification that you need to in order to understand what they want. You do not want to have to come back to your boss again regarding the same matter!

Example:

(Knock gently on the boss's door; or ask an appointment).

Ms. Combs, I'm sorry to bother you but I have a question that I have not been able to get resolved on my own. I have re-read the manuals you gave me and I talked with Joe. If you have a minute, can you give me some guidance about what you'd like me to do. I want to be sure I get it right for you. I'll take notes if you don't mind.

(Then, explain the situation as briefly as you can. Allow your boss to ask questions, if he or she needs to).

(Follow up later with your boss, thanking them for the guidance and letting him or her know you were able to resolve the matter).

WHO: No Relationship Ranking

This would not be applicable most of the time. You will likely have a low relationship ranking with a boss. However, if you are working for someone you have never met before, such as working on assignment away from home, or working with new clients or coworkers, use the rules for the Low Relationship Ranking.

In an Emergency

In an emergency, ask anyone who can help that is near you. For example, if you have broken something or something you are responsible for is lost, missing, or stolen, ask the coworkers immediately around you to help—this is preferable to being fired. Report the incident to your boss if it could not be resolved. It is likely someone else will report it to him or her, anyway. Bosses do not like to be surprised. It is better for you to tell the boss that you did something wrong, such as break or lose something, than for another co-worker to tell.

WHAT/Purpose:

I think my boss is upset with me.

HOW: *Pick the one based on the person's relationship ranking.*

WHO: High Relationship Ranking

 See Medium or Low Relationship Ranking. In the event that you work for a relative or loved one and have high relationship ranking, you'll still want to use the formal register (behave professionally) when on the job. Use the strategies below to find just the right approach.

WHO: Medium Relationship Ranking

If you are fairly familiar with your boss, a direct and honest approach is best. The better you know him or her, the more likely he or she is to know your strengths and challenges. At this medium (or possibly high) relationship ranking, I recommend sharing the personal story of what went wrong or why you failed, rather than just saying the facts. He or she might be more forgiving and understanding if you're honest. Just use the formal register and demonstrate with your words and actions that you intend to improve your performance. For example, perhaps you are babysitting for a friend of the family or you have been hired by your uncle's lawn company, you may want to share more about what went wrong. In the end, you should seek guidance from your employer and accept that his or her opinion is important to you—and really the only opinion that matters when you need to keep your job.

Example:

Mr. Koch, I know you wanted to see me. How might I be able to help you?

(Mr. Koch says that he is disappointed with your recent performance).

Well, Mr. Koch, I am so sorry that you are disappointed. My job here with you is very important to me and I want you to be pleased with my work. Can we make a list of the things that I need to do to improve? I'll take some notes and follow up with you later about what I am doing to improve in each of the areas you name. Would that be okay?

(Mr. Koch will probably then explain the specifics of his concerns).

(Repeat back to Mr. Koch what you believe he has told you about what you need to do to improve. You may summarize what he has said into a short list of immediate and long-term actions. Seek his agreement by asking, *"Does that sound about right, sir?"*)

(Close the conversation by thanking your employer for the chance to correct your performance and the advice that he or she has given you. Follow up by sending a brief e-mail to the boss explaining what you intend to do to improve.)

WHO: Low Relationship Ranking

Approaching a boss with whom you have a low relationship ranking will likely look very much the same as the with medium relationship ranking, so use the description and examples given there to get started. However, sometimes, employers with a low relationship ranking may not be as friendly toward you, may even be hostile toward you when speaking to you. They may be angry, or even mean. When this happens, maintain your politeness and formal register. If your job is important to you, you may have to accept criticism that is not very nice and talking back to your boss with harsh words will not go well. This is a person who can fire you.

You may also want to get to know the worker's rights laws in your area. Knowing what rights to appeal when defending yourself may be important. Whatever you do, document what happened in some private notes and follow up with your boss about your progress toward improving. Sometimes, being assertive and positive can disarm an angry boss. Whatever you do, be humble and respectful. Show and say that you are seeking help. Be ready to analyze and improve your performance.

WHO: No Relationship Ranking

This would not be applicable. You will at least have a low relationship ranking with a boss.

In an Emergency

If your performance on the job has created an emergency, you will have to be prepared to hear how your boss is disappointed with you in the middle of that emergency—it may involve him or her yelling at you in a high pressure situation. Try to accept the yelling, as best you can, and find out from your boss what you need to do to repair the situation. Follow up after the emergency is resolved, either in-person or by e-mail, telling your boss how sorry you are, and how you intend to prevent the emergency in the future.

WHAT/Purpose:

I have received a letter stating that I have done something wrong.

This situation is like the one above; the difference is that you received the negative feedback from your boss in writing. This is an important difference because when someone gets negative feedback from a boss in writing it means that the boss is probably starting a process that can lead to you getting fired. Employers, by law and/or by company policy, have to make written efforts to provide you opportunities to fix your performance. Often, when a first letter of warning is written to you, it is serious—you need to drastically improve your performance in order to avoid further warnings and being fired. Get help from a loved one, not a coworker. When a second letter of warning is issued, you may want to seek legal advice. Beyond that, here are some basic approaches.

HOW: *Pick the one based on the person's relationship ranking.*

WHO: High Relationship Ranking

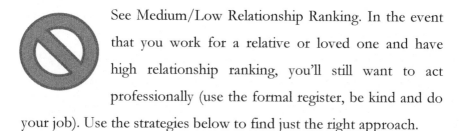

See Medium/Low Relationship Ranking. In the event that you work for a relative or loved one and have high relationship ranking, you'll still want to act professionally (use the formal register, be kind and do your job). Use the strategies below to find just the right approach.

WHO: Medium Relationship Ranking

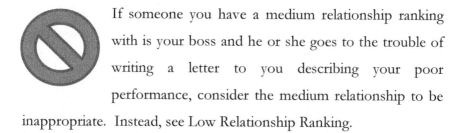

If someone you have a medium relationship ranking with is your boss and he or she goes to the trouble of writing a letter to you describing your poor performance, consider the medium relationship to be inappropriate. Instead, see Low Relationship Ranking.

WHO: Low Relationship Ranking

No matter what your previous relationship with this person is, you need to treat this situation very formally. This is serious. When receiving a letter about your poor performance, you need to act! You will need to meet with the person who lodged the complaint against you. Before going to the meeting, get help from a parent, a loved one, or a good friend for help planning for the meeting. The second time, seek help from a union representative (if the industry has one) or a lawyer who is an expert in worker's rights. Be sure that that person is aware of your Asperger's. You should respond to the letter in writing (it can be an e-mail) and have a face-to-face meeting with your employer. Depending on the company policy, you may or may not have a support person (someone who will help you) in the room with you. See the previous situation, *I think my boss is upset with me*, for an example of how the initial meeting should go. You may need to meet more than once if the situation is difficult or complicated. The meeting will probably result in some demands by your boss.

Example

At the meeting, after greeting your boss politely, you may want to do the following things:

1. Express your concern, e.g. *"I am anxious to do what you need me to do. I want to improve the situation."*
2. Ask for help, e.g. *"Can you help me with what I have done wrong?"* Ask questions if you don't understand.
3. Clarify steps for improvement, e.g. *"Can we write this down as a plan for me to follow?"* If he or she won't do it or asks you to do it, write down a plan. Ask the boss to check it.

4. <u>Ask for follow up</u>, e.g. *"May I check in with you periodically to see how you think that I'm doing?"* Ask how often he or she would like to see you for follow up.

WHO: No Relationship Ranking

This would not apply. You will at least have a low relationship ranking with a boss.

In an Emergency

While the letter you receive may be the result of an emergency you created, it will not be written during the emergency. See Low Relationship Ranking for this situation.

WHAT/Purpose:

I have to attend a special event and don't know how to introduce myself and make conversation.

HOW: *Pick the one based on the person's relationship ranking.*

WHO: High Relationship Ranking

1. State the person's first name.

2. Smile broadly.

3. "Good to see you!"

4. Shake hands.

5. Ask them something about the evening like who they came with or where they are sitting.

Example:

"George!

(Make a broad smile).

"So good to see you!"

(Shake hands).

"Did you come by yourself to this?"

WHO: Medium Relationship Ranking

1. Start by stating the person's name.

2. Smile.

3. Ask how the person is.

4. Shake hands, then ask them something about the evening like who they came with or where they are sitting.

Example:

"Hi, Lisa!

(Smile).

"How are you?"

(Shake hands)

"Have you been looking forward to this?"

WHO: Low Relationship Ranking

1. Greet the person.
2. State your name, if necessary.
3. Ask how the person is.
4. Shake hands, then ask them something about the evening like who they came with or where they are sitting.

Example:

"Hello."

"I don't know if you remember me...I'm Rick Smith."

"It is nice to see you. How are you?"

WHO: No Relationship Ranking

1. Greet the person.

2. Offer your hand to shake.

3. State your name.

4. Then ask them something about his or her participation in the evening.

Example:

"Hello."

(Offer a handshake). *"It's nice to meet you."*

"My name is James Carver. What's yours?"

(Pause to wait for the name).

"Are you presenting tonight?"

In an Emergency

This kind of an "emergency" might not be a real emergency. It may be that you need something urgently for your presentation or you do not know where you are supposed to be.

1. Make a polite introduction.

2. State your name and role at the event.

3. Ask for help.

Example:

"Excuse me. My name is Sam White. I am supposed to be at the presenter's table. Can you help me?"

WHAT/Purpose:

I have to present my ideas to a group of people.

HOW: *Pick the one based on the person's relationship ranking.*

Speaking in front of an audience is most people's greatest fear, even for folks without Asperger's; so, don't feel bad if you are nervous or afraid. It is a really natural feeling. The important thing to remember is that when you are asked to present something, it is probably because someone thinks you have something really important to say. Remember this when you feel embarrassed or anxious. The message is the most important thing. If your hands shake or your face turns red, the audience usually cannot tell. Most people know how scary presenting can be. They will be kind and will want to see you succeed. Here are some ideas to help you feel less nervous:

1. Come to the presentation as prepared as you can. Plan out what you will say, at the beginning middle and end of your

speech. Feel free to bring notes (just don't depend on them too much). I find using some technology, like a slide presentation helps me stay focused and gives the audience something to look at besides me. If you do use notes, have them on something small like cards. Don't write out the whole speech or you will be tempted to read it word for word, which is not good. Simply write reminders, such as in a bulleted list of the important things you want to say. As you make each point, read the card quickly to remind yourself of what you want to say, look up and say in your own words what you want to say.

2. Practice. Practice. Practice. Practice by yourself in front of a mirror; practice with a friend or family member who has a high familiarity ranking; or, practice with a trusted co-worker or former teacher or mentor. You will be able to shake some of your nerves by getting a feel for what your voice sounds like and what it feels like to look at people when you are speaking. Seek advice from the people you practice in front of.

3. During the presentation, find a couple of familiar or kind faces in the audience. Try to find several people that are in different places in the audience so that you will not be tempted to look at the same person during the entire presentation.

* If you are really not comfortable giving a speech, talk to your boss before the presentation about your fears. Ask if there is anything else you could do besides a "speech" that would be acceptable, such as a panel discussion with other speakers standing alongside of you, or a digital presentation that might allow you to broadcast the presentation by recording your voice over some digital slides that can be sent to the audience on e-mail, etc.

WHO: High/Medium Relationship Ranking

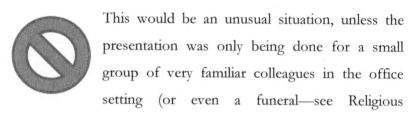 This would be an unusual situation, unless the presentation was only being done for a small group of very familiar colleagues in the office setting (or even a funeral—see Religious settings). In this case, ask if you can be seated during the presentation so that you can be comfortable. Bring handouts or something for the audience to look at while you are speaking.

WHO: Low Relationship Ranking

The examples below will help you in most public speaking situations. With all presentations, you must have in introduction, major points with examples or details, and a conclusion.

Steps to <u>introduce</u> a presentation:

1. Get your audience's attention that relates to the subject matter. Attention getters can include a quote, a fact or statistic, a story, or simply telling them that you're glad to be with them and why what you're going to speak about is so important to you.

2. Provide a main idea (sometimes called a thesis statement) that tells them the most important reason you are speaking with them.

3. Preview what they are about to hear from you.

Example of an Introduction:

This is an example of an introduction for a speech about new invention. Notice the "attention getter" is in the form of a question and a fact. Attention getters can also be quotes, stories, statistic/facts, or jokes:

"How many of you have ever found yourself spending many additional hours after doing your laundry trying to find the mates to all of your socks? Did you know that the average household of three has over 100 pairs of socks between them and sorting and pairing those socks before and after cleaning can consume more time than 70 minutes of your laundry day? The product I will introduce to you today will end all of those wasted hours by helping you keep your socks paired throughout the wash and dry cycle. I will begin my presentation by demonstrating my product, then discuss how cost effective the product is."

Your conclusion should include a summary of what you have just presented, and in a meaningful way, return to the attention getter.

Example of a Conclusion:

"As you can see, my product fastens socks together easily, without causing holes or stretching. Most importantly, it will save the average household hours of wasted time sorting and pairing socks!"

The body of your presentation should contain only the facts and details that are important to your main idea or thesis. While you may love the scientific process behind your product or topic, your audience may not, and they only need to hear what the idea means to them.

WHO: No Relationship Ranking

Directions for making a presentation in front of people with whom you have no relationship ranking can follow the examples above—just add to the introduction (see above) your name, your job and perhaps some experience that you have which lends credibility to why you are the best person to make the presentation.

Example of an Addition to the Introduction:

"Good morning, my name is Alex. I am an inventor and engineer. I believe I have a product that will save you hundreds of hours in labor over the course of your life!"

In an Emergency

Sometimes, you may have to make a presentation in an emergency. For example, perhaps your boss puts you in charge of the public address (P.A.) system when he is not at the office. You could be asked to make emergency announcements.

Example:

(If in person, place your hands in the air and speak loudly. If doing this over the public address system, be brief, use a calm voice and repeat the announcement twice).

"I apologize for the interruption! I have an important announcement."

(Name the type of emergency and give specific directions on what people should do.)

Toolkit Worksheet

What are other situations that you have found to be an issue? Name the situation here and determine your plan. Return here later and report what you actually said. (See p. 128 for directions on how to use this worksheet).

WHO: _____**Relationship Ranking**_____

WHAT (purpose):_____

WHERE: _____

   Hidden Rules? If yes, what?_____

_____

HOW (describe below):

What I plan to say (can I use the basic strategy? Y/N):

What I actually said (to be filled in later):

Describe the difference and why (to be filled in later):

WHERE: STORE/BANK

Special Note: Use the formal register only, except as noted.

WHAT/Purpose:

I am applying for or asking for something at a business and an employee was rude/short with me.

Sometimes, when you have Asperger's, it is difficult to tell if someone is being rude to you. You may need to practice with a loved one. Get help learning what angry, sad, happy, annoyed, tired and other facial expressions look like. There are many picture-based diagrams on the internet that can help you begin to look for the typical expressions and what moods they represent. You can search *images* under "mood charts," "charts to help recognize mood," "feelings charts," "mood faces," or other combinations of words like these to find one to get you started. But practicing on real people's faces is best.

HOW: *Pick the one based on the person's relationship ranking.*

WHO: High Relationship Ranking

This would be an unusual situation unless the employee was a close friend or family member. However, if it did happen, you might attempt to simply ask if everything is okay.

Example:

"Juanita, what's up? Anything wrong?"

WHO: Medium Relationship Ranking

If the person has a medium relationship ranking, the approach above may be the best, just said with a little more formality.

Example:

"John, you seem tense today. Is anything wrong? If this isn't a good time, I can come back later."

WHO: Low/No Relationship Ranking

This category is where you are most likely to see unpleasant or rude behavior. The first thing you want to consider here is whether it is worth it to demand that they change their attitude. Sometimes simply tolerating minor rudeness is acceptable or you may want to see if someone else can help you, like in the examples below:

Example:

"Is there someone else who can help me?"

(OR if they persist in being rude...)

"I would like to speak to your manager, please."

In an Emergency

When there are emergencies people often forget their best manners; that's okay. Just focus on what you need to get out of the situation. Disregard the behaviors.

Example:

"Stop! I really do need help. If you can't help me then get someone who can!"

WHAT/Purpose:

I need some help.

See General Settings/Anywhere.

Toolkit Worksheet

What are other situations that you have found to be an issue? Name the situation here and determine your plan. Return here later and report what you actually said. (See p. 128 for directions on how to use this worksheet).

WHO: _____**Relationship Ranking**_____

WHAT (purpose):_____

WHERE: _____

Hidden Rules? If yes, what?_____

_____

HOW (describe below):

What I plan to say (can I use the basic strategy? Y/N):

What I actually said (to be filled in later):

Describe the difference and why (to be filled in later):

Julie Hutchins Koch, Ph.D.

WHERE:
RELIGIOUS SETTINGS

Special Note: Because religious settings and situations are places of worship, most people will expect you to use the formal register only, at least during religious services. At social events at any of these locations (or even in the home when there is a religious situation), a less formal register should be acceptable.

WHAT/Purpose:

I've been asked to offer a prayer.

HOW: *Pick the one based on the person's relationship ranking.*

WHO: High/Medium/Low Relationship Ranking

Even in a high relationship ranking, religious situations will still need a certain amount of formality, especially when you are speaking to the presiding "clergy" (religious leader). Speak with a parent or someone with whom you have a high relationship ranking about how to do this. If you are not comfortable, it is okay to say no, politely (such as, *"Would you mind having someone else say the prayer?"*).

The basics of prayer include an address to God, giving thanks, asking for special needs, and a closing. The closing can be different based on the religion, but typically a simple "amen" will do.

Example of a Christian Prayer:

"Dear Heavenly Father, we thank you for the food we are about to receive. Please bless the people here today. In Jesus name we pray, Amen."

No example is given for Jewish or Islamic prayer examples, as they would typically include some recitations. Check with your local religious leaders or family on what would be an appropriate method of prayer.

WHO: No Relationship Ranking or In an Emergency

 It is difficult to imagine a scenario in which you would be praying with a stranger unless you were in a setting that required it of you, such as a prayer group, a hotline, or if you were in a true emergency where people were seeking urgent emotional comfort. If that is the case, simply pray the best way you know how: address God, ask for what you need, and close with an Amen!

WHAT/Purpose:

I've been invited to go to a religious service with a friend who is a different religion than me.

HOW: *Pick the one based on the person's relationship ranking.*

WHO: High/Medium Relationship Ranking

As I said earlier in the special note for this section, even in high relationship ranking, religious situations will call for a certain amount of formality, especially when speaking to the presiding clergy. Before going to the service, talk with the friend or family member who invited you about what you might expect (including what to wear). Ask if you may sit next to them during the service so that they can give you guidance throughout the service.

Typically, you will be expected to be quiet or reverent and follow some simple directions, such as singing assigned hymns (songs), recitations, or prayers. The bottom line is that if everyone stands up, you stand up; if everyone kneels, you kneel (if you have any physical impairments or there are other people not following along, you may choose).

If you are in a church that gives "communion" (taking of a sacramental bread/cracker and water/wine), ask in advance if you should/can take it. Some churches invite all congregants to partake in the ceremony, others do not. If you do not participate, be sure you move clear of others who are participating. If you choose to participate, stay close to the person with whom you went to the service and follow his or her lead.

WHO: Low/No Relationship Ranking or In an Emergency

 It may not be likely that you would be asked to go to a service in any of the above situations. If for some reason you are, consult with a loved or someone with a high/medium relationship ranking prior to going about what you might expect. See Medium/High Relationship Ranking for details.

WHAT/Purpose:

I am going to a funeral.

There are some basic things that have to happen at a funeral that you will want to be aware of. For example, sometimes, you may be asked to view the body. You will likely need to hug or shake the hand of the family whose loved one has died. You may even be a member of the family whose loved one has died and be expected to do certain things for the special services at the funeral, memorial, or viewing.

People may expect things from you that are very hard for you and that may not even come naturally to you. You may also have to go to several locations that are hard to handle, such as a church, a funeral home and a cemetery. The most important thing to remember is that when someone has died, emotions are very high. Behaving in ways that show you care, that show that you understand how others feel, and that make things easier on those most affected by the death are really important to your closest relationships.

HOW: *Pick the one based on the person's relationship ranking.*

WHO: High/Medium Relationship Ranking

Again, even with a high relationship ranking, funerals will always require a certain amount of formality, especially when speaking to the clergy and the spouse and children of the deceased. Prior to going, speak with the close friend or family member about what you might expect. Ask your friend if you may sit next to them during the service so that they can give you guidance throughout the service, at the funeral home, the church and the cemetery. Typically, you will be expected to be quiet and reverent at all times and follow some simple directions, songs, or prayers.

One event that almost always happens at a funeral is that people line up to give their "condolences" to the family of the deceased.

To give condolences:

1. Shake the hand of each person in the line,
2. Offer a gentle hug.
3. Say something comforting to the person (see examples below).

Examples:

"I'm so sorry for your loss."

AND/OR

"Please let me know if there is anything I can do."

AND/OR

"We all really loved him."

AND/OR

"Please know that I am here for you."

WHO: Low/No Relationship Rankin or In an Emergency

 It may not be likely that you would be asked to go to the funeral of anyone in these situations. However, if for some reason you are, consult with a loved or someone with a high/medium relationship ranking prior to going about what you might expect and what you might need to do. One important note here would be that if you are going to a service for someone you don't know, such as might be expected at your place of employment, hugging is not appropriate.

Toolkit Worksheet

What are other situations that you have found to be an issue? Name the situation here and determine your plan. Return here later and report what you actually said. (See p. 128 for directions on how to use this worksheet).

WHO: _____**Relationship Ranking**_____

WHAT (purpose):_____

WHERE: _____

Hidden Rules? If yes, what?_____

_____

HOW (describe below):

What I plan to say (can I use the basic strategy? Y/N):

What I actually said (to be filled in later):

Describe the difference and why (to be filled in later):

WHERE: LEGAL SETTINGS

COURT ROOM, ATTORNEY'S OFFICE, POLICE STATION, ETC.

While I hope that you will not have an occasion to see an attorney, go to court, or have to meet with the police, it can happen. Sometimes you may need to be there to support someone else; sometimes you may be a witness; sometimes you may have legal documents that need to be handled for property or civil matters; hopefully, you will not be there because you have done something wrong!

Regardless of why you go to court, meet with a lawyer or see the police always use the formal register. These situations are serious and require respectful attention and no interruptions. So, don't speak, unless you are asked to. If you are the subject of the legal proceeding and feel like something needs to be said, and you feel like no one is saying it, consult with your lawyer before speaking.

There are only a couple of situations in this section because so many legal situations are case specific. Use the Toolkit worksheet with a loved one, your lawyer, or someone with a high relationship ranking to help you sort through situations that you can plan for prior to going to court, or attending a deposition (big word, but if it happens, you'll be told what that means).

WHAT/Purpose:

Someone asked me a question that makes me want to cry.

It is an awful feeling when you want to cry and you have no privacy. Here is some help.

HOW: *Pick the one based on the person's relationship ranking.*

WHO: High Relationship Ranking

 This would be unusual, unless your friend or family member is your attorney.

WHO: Medium Relationship Ranking

 This would be reserved for an attorney that you have known a long time and you can use the low or no relationship guidance to help you.

WHO: Low/No Relationship Ranking

1. Ask for a moment to stop. You will likely not be permitted to leave, but you can ask for help.

2. Ask for a tissue, a quiet moment, or to speak with your attorney or a loved one alone.

3. Focus on why you are there and take a few deep breaths.

4. Once you are calmer, you can tell the attorney or judge that you are ready to begin again.

Example:

"Your honor. May I stop for a moment?"

(Wait for the judge to reply).

"May I have a tissue?"

"Would it be okay to speak with" (name the person)."

(Later when you feel better, say):

"I'm ready to proceed."

In an Emergency

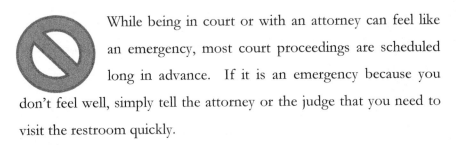

While being in court or with an attorney can feel like an emergency, most court proceedings are scheduled long in advance. If it is an emergency because you don't feel well, simply tell the attorney or the judge that you need to visit the restroom quickly.

WHAT/Purpose:

I am driving my car and I have been pulled over by the police. What do I do?

It can be scary to be pulled over by the police, even when you have done nothing wrong. Here is some help. Don't get too upset; while you may feel like it is the end of the world, it is not. Most of the time, if you get a ticket from an officer, it can be resolved by paying a fine, and/or going to court. The more calm you can be, the better result you will have. Do not yell, curse at, or physically touch the officer. Keep your hands where the officer can see them, such as on the steering wheel. Follow the officer's instruction if he or she asks you to step out of the car or produce your driver's license.

HOW: *Pick the one based on the person's relationship ranking.*

WHO: High/Medium Relationship Ranking:

This would be unusual, unless the police officer is a friend or family member.

WHO: Low/No Relationship Ranking

1. Pull over in a safe location as quickly as possible.

2. Roll down your window and place your hands on the steering wheel. Stay seated in the car. Wait for the officer to approach your vehicle; this may take a moment as he or she looks up information about your license plate so be patient.

3. When the officer approaches you, greet him or her. Listen to what the officer has to say. Produce whatever documentation he asks for, usually this will be your driver's license and proof of insurance.

4. If you are asked questions, answer him or her briefly and truthfully; although, if you don't know the answer to a question, you may say, "*I didn't/don't know.*"

5. If the officer cites you for a violation, he or she will give you some papers describing the violation and who you may contact when responding to the violation. Quickly look over these papers and ask the officer any questions you may have.

Example:

(With your hands on the steering wheel.)

"Hello, Officer."

(Wait for the officer to reply. Briefly answer his or her question. Then…)

"Are you going to give me a ticket?"

(Listen while the officer tells you what is going to happen. Ask any questions you may have):

"Do I have to appear in court or is this a fine only?"

(Listen while the officer explains. Ask any questions you may have):

"Can you show me on the ticket where I can find out more information about who I can speak to about this?"

(Listen while the officer responds).

"Thank you. Is that all?

(Listen while the officer responds).

"Goodbye."

In an Emergency

If you are being pulled over by a police officer in an emergency, some of what is suggested above may not be appropriate. If there is a car fire, an accident, or the officer asks you to get out of your car, follow all directions very quickly, but do not provide more information than just your name and any documentation asked for. As soon as you are able call a trusted friend or family member to ask for help. If there is no police officer and there is a car fire, or an accident, call 911 and get help immediately!

Toolkit Worksheet

What are other situations that you have found to be an issue? Name the situation here and determine your plan. Return here later and report what you actually said. (See p. 128 for directions on how to use this worksheet).

WHO: _____ **Relationship Ranking** _____

WHAT (purpose): _____

WHERE: _____

Hidden Rules? If yes, what? _____

_____

HOW (describe below):

What I plan to say (can I use the basic strategy? Y/N):

What I actually said (to be filled in later):

Describe the difference and why (to be filled in later):

WHERE: ANYWHERE
AND OTHER GENERAL SETTINGS

Special Note: Because the following situations can take place anywhere, the formality needed may change depending on the person's relationship ranking.

WHAT/Purpose:

I think I hurt someone's feelings.

HOW: *Pick the one based on the person's relationship ranking.*

WHO: High Relationship Ranking

While hurting the feelings of someone you are very close to is more painful than hurting anyone else in your life, it can be easier to share your feelings with someone you are very close to.

1. Start by stating the person's first name
2. Share a sincere apology.
3. Explain your actions. You can be very personal with someone you whose high on the Relationship Ranking Scale™ .
4. Propose a long-term solution.

Example:

"Dad, I am so sorry I hurt your feelings. I think I was feeling overtired and I wasn't paying attention. You know how I get when I am overtired. Next time I'm feeling this way, I'll just tell you that I'm too tired to do anything."

WHO: Medium Relationship Ranking

1. Start by stating the person's first name
2. Share a sincere apology based on what you think you did to hurt them.
3. Explain your actions. You can be very personal with someone high on the Relationship Ranking Scale™ .
4. Propose a long-term solution.

Example:

"Jeff, I am really sorry if I said anything that hurt your feelings. I think I was just really overtired. Next time I'm feeling this way, I'll just tell you directly."

OR

"Jeff, I just wasn't thinking. I didn't mean to be unkind. Please accept my apology. I'll try not do it again.

WHO: Low/No Relationship Ranking

While you can hurt someone's feelings anywhere, this section is for people who will be in your home. This would not usually be found in the home unless a guest or solicitor was at the home.

In an Emergency

While there can be emergencies in your home, repairing hurt feelings during an emergency is not a priority. See important definitions regarding what is considered an emergency.

WHAT/Purpose:

I really like someone in a romantic way and I don't
know how to tell them.

Special Note: See also Special Feature: Falling in Love, later in the book.

HOW: *Pick the one based on the person's relationship ranking.*

WHO: High Relationship Ranking

Revealing your secret feelings to someone you already know very well can sometimes be harder than telling someone you hardly know; it can feel this way because there is so much more to risk when we say something that might change a relationship we want to keep. In other words, telling a close friend that you like them in a romantic way may result in the close friend not returning your feelings. This can sometimes make your close friend feel differently about you, or worry that you will always want to be romantic with them. If you choose to tell a close friend that you have romantic feelings for them now, be sure that your feelings are strong enough to risk the relationship changing in some way. This kind of conversation is done best in person, but if you're too nervous, you can do it by phone. Do not do this by text or e-mail.

1. State the person's first name or the name you usually call him or her. Unlike most high relationship rankings where I tell you that you do not need to use their name in the basic communication strategy, I want you to say the name here. This will let them know that you're about to say something important.

2. Say that you want to have a serious conversation; this will prepare them to focus on what you're about to say. Ask if they have time to have the conversation.

3. State your feelings in a simple way. State both your feelings for the friendship and for the person.

4. Let your friend know that it is not important that they respond now; this will give them time to think about it and let them know that you care about how they feel about what you've said.

5. Suggest that you either end the conversation so that you can both think or that you do something "normal" that you would normally do as friends; this will let your friend now that you are not pressuring them to respond or decide how they feel.

Example:

"Holly, I wanted to talk to you about something really important. Do you have a minute? I wanted to talk to you about us. Your friendship means so much to me and we have so much fun together. I hope you don't mind me telling you that I care about you as more than a friend. If you feel the same way, I'd really like that. You don't have to tell me your feelings about this now. I just wanted you to

know how I felt. Whatever happens I hope we can be friends. Would you like to get together later to talk about this or do you want to just go do something fun?"

WHO: Medium Relationship Ranking

Someone with whom you have a medium relationship ranking can create some difficulty in how and when to decide to tell someone you have special feelings for them. There are many reasons and many ways we might have a "medium" relationship ranking. In this situation, these people would be good friends or a roommate with whom you feel safe and good. Depending on who they are, you may be using the formal or informal register with them. The register you use can change the way you might say this important thing to your friend, but you'll want to be very respectful and hold back from sharing all of your feelings until you know that it is safe. If the person has a medium ranking because you had to subtract points in the special scoring section of the Relationship Ranking Scale, you do not want to share your feelings. Go speak with a trusted friend or adult about why you have romantic feelings for someone who has the potential to hurt your feelings.

You will basically follow the same steps you would if you were saying this to someone who has a high relationship ranking with you, just a bit more carefully.

Remember that words in *italics* (slanted writing) are the actual words I suggest you say. If it is not in *italics*, they are just additional steps, or actions you should consider.

Example:

"Loren, I wanted to talk to you about something. Do you have time to talk?"

(Once they have confirmed they do, invite them to sit some place comfortable. Then, continue.)

"It has been really nice getting to know you and become good friends. You are great. I have been thinking about you a lot lately and wanted you to ask if you would ever be interested in going out sometime—just you and me. You don't have to answer me now, but I just wanted to tell you that I have feelings for you that are more than just friends. What do you think? Do you want to talk about it now, or do you want to get together later to talk more?"

WHO: Low/No Relationship Ranking

There is some risk in deciding that you like someone who ranks low on the Relationship Ranking Scale. However, a few times in your life, you may meet someone that you do not know very well but would like to get to know better. It is okay to take a chance and ask them to spend more time with you; however, be careful about how much of your feelings you express to this person in the moment. You will want to gradually increase your trust (or relationship ranking) with the person before you share all of your feelings. Of course, if the person has a low ranking because you had to subtract points in the special scoring section of the Relationship Ranking Scale, you will not want to share your feelings. Go speak with a trusted friend or adult about why you have romantic feelings for someone who has the potential to hurt your feelings.

1. Compliment the person and be specific (other than a compliment about their body).

2. Find out a little about their situation.

3. Determine whether they are in a relationship with someone else, before expressing your feelings. If they are in a relationship, it is best to hold back on expressing yourself. If they are not in a relationship, you can, with some caution, proceed to explore the possibility of spending more time with them.

Example:

"You are great, Emily. Your sense of humor is awesome. I'd love to spend more time with you. Are you free to hang out sometime?"

In an Emergency

 This is not an appropriate time to share your feelings about someone or to try to see if they are in a relationship. The emergency must be handled first. See Important Definitions regarding what is considered an emergency.

WHAT/Purpose:

I want to talk about something that no one else is talking about or change the subject.

When you want to introduce a new topic of conversation, think of something that connects the topic with the current topic you'd like to introduce. Then, you can say something like, "Speaking of [mention the first topic]," or "Did you know [mention your topic]." If you can't think of a simple connection, then your topic may need to wait until a later time. Be mindful that if there is a situation with high emotion, switching topics is never appropriate. Also, remember that if the person does not want to talk about the subject you bring up they may not tell you; they may make an unpleasant face (wrinkle their nose, face the palm of their hand out to you, or say something like "don't go there," or "whatever." If this happens, drop the topic!

HOW: *Pick the one based on the person's relationship ranking.*

WHO: High Relationship Ranking

Example:

"Speaking of _____ *did you know ....?"* (add something that was being discussed already)

213

WHO: Medium Relationship Ranking

Example:

"I don't mean to change the subject but I heard something interesting today that I thought you might be interested in."

WHO: Low Relationship Ranking

Example:

"I know this is not what we were talking about but I read something today that I thought you might be interested in?"

WHO: No Relationship Ranking

Example:

"Excuse me, may I mention something different from what we've been talking about?"

In an Emergency

Example:

"Please listen! I must say something!"

WHAT/Purpose:

I don't understand what is being asked of me.

HOW: *Pick the one based on the person's relationship ranking.*

The basic approach for all of these examples is:

1. Make a polite interruption.
2. State why you are confused.
3. Ask for help.

WHO: High Relationship Ranking

Example:

"Hey, I don't get it. Can you show me?"

WHO: Medium Relationship Ranking

Example:

"I have just one question, if you have a minute. I don't understand. Can you go over it again?"

WHO: Low Relationship Ranking

Example:

"Excuse me. This is a bit confusing. Can you explain this again?"

WHO: No Relationship Ranking

Example:

"Pardon me. Can you explain this in more detail?"

In an Emergency

Example:

"Please help! I can't do it!"

WHAT/Purpose:

I need help.

HOW: *Pick the one based on the person's relationship ranking.*

The basic approach for all of these examples is:

1. Make a polite interruption or state the person's name.
2. State what you need.
3. Ask for help.

WHO: High Relationship Ranking

Example:

"Mom, I'm having trouble getting this open. Help me out, would you?"

WHO: Medium Relationship Ranking

Example:

"Emma, I can't find that book. Do you think you could help me?"

WHO: Low Relationship Ranking

Example:

"Sorry to bother you, sir. I need a new form. Could you help me, please?"

WHO: No Relationship Ranking

Example:

"Excuse me, ma'am. I need to reach that shelf. Do you mind letting me by?"

In an Emergency

Example:

"Help! I need help!"

WHAT/Purpose:
Someone is yelling at me.

HOW: *Pick the one based on the person's relationship ranking.*

The basic approach for all of these examples is:

1. Make a polite interruption.
2. Name what is happening.
3. Ask to talk about the situation later.

WHO: High Relationship Ranking

Example:

"I know you're upset, but yelling at me won't help. Let's talk about this later."

WHO: Medium Relationship Ranking

Example:

"Wait a minute. I know you're angry. But can we talk about this calmly?"

WHO: Low Relationship Ranking

Example:

"Excuse me. I can see that you're upset. I think it would be better if we speak when you're more calm."

WHO: No Relationship Ranking

Example:

"Excuse me. Please don't speak to me that way. I'll come back later."

In an Emergency

Example:

"Wait! What's wrong? Why are you yelling?"

WHAT/Purpose:

Someone I know is happy, but I don't understand why.

HOW: *Pick the one based on the person's relationship ranking.*

The basic approach for all of these examples is:

1. Acknowledge what you see.
2. Ask a question.
3. Offer congratulations.

WHO: High Relationship Ranking

Example:

(Say this while smiling broadly and perhaps offer a hug).

"You seem really happy. What's up?

(Wait for a response, and if appropriate, say):

"I'm so happy for you."

WHO: Medium Relationship Ranking

Example:

(Say this while smiling broadly).

"That's quite a grin you have! Did you get some good news?

(Wait for a response, and if appropriate, say):

"Great news!"

WHO: Low Relationship Ranking

Example:

"You seem so happy. Did you get some good news?"

(Wait for a response, and if appropriate, say):

"Good for you! Congratulations!"

OR

"I'm glad to see you so happy!"

WHO: No Relationship Ranking

 It would not be wise to ask someone who you do not know why they are smiling. It may be seen as rude.

In an Emergency

 This is not applicable.

WHAT/Purpose:

I have received a compliment/commendation.

You might think it is strange to talk about what to do when things go well, and not just when they go wrong. What you must remember is that when people take the time to compliment you or award you something, the verbal and nonverbal reactions you have to what they have said, done or written will matter to them. Indeed, people can have their feelings hurt when the time and attention they have paid to you is not recognized by you properly. People may feel you are ungrateful or don't care about what they think if you do not show your appreciation. Worse, if you don't show them enough appreciation, you are less likely to receive compliments or commendations in the future—and these can be important for moving ahead at work. So what do you do? Read below:

HOW: *Pick the one based on the person's relationship ranking.*

WHO: High Relationship Ranking

When someone you know very well compliments you, they are sincerely hoping that you will "feel" that compliment; and, because they can't see inside your head or your heart you will need to say or do something to show you have felt their love and appreciation.

Example 1:

(Your best friend tells you that he really likes your new shoes).

(You can say something like):

"Thanks, man. I worked hard to pay for these. I'm glad you noticed."

Example 2:

(Your girlfriend tells you that you have beautiful eyes).

(Say something like):

"Thank you, sweetheart. You are so beautiful to me, too."

(You can follow up with a hug, a kiss or a tender touch of her face).

Example 3:

(Your grandmother gives you $50 as she says goodbye to you on your way back to college, saying):

"You are doing a great job, kiddo. Use this to treat yourself."

(You should say something like):

"Grandma, thank you so much. You didn't have to do this, but I appreciate your support of me every day! I love you. I'll use the money wisely."

(Be sure your response includes a hug for her!).

WHO: Medium/Low Relationship Ranking

Even with medium to low relationship rankings, people want to know that their kind words or deeds toward you meant something to you.

1. Smile.
2. Say, "Thank you," OR "I appreciate that."
3. Offer a handshake.
4. Consider making a compliment in return.

Example for receiving a **plaque or certificate** thanking you for your service at work:

When receiving this in a public forum, such as a stage or in front of a group of people,

(Smile. Then, say something like):

"Thank you for your kind recognition of me. I really appreciate it. So many of you helped me to achieve this and I hope you will accept it with me."

(Shake the hand of those immediately around you then walk out of the center of attention, perhaps standing to the side, or walking off of the stage).

When receiving this in private or with just a couple of people around,

(Smile. Then, say something like):

"Thanks a lot. I really appreciate it."

(Shake the hand of those immediately around you then walk out of the center of attention, perhaps standing to the side, or returning to work, depending on what others are doing at that time).

WHO: No Relationship Ranking

While strangers or people who fall in this ranking are not as likely to offer a compliment to you, it does happen. Use the opportunity to practice your social skills. The best and most direct approach is to say: *Thank you! I appreciate that very much.*

In an Emergency

 This is not applicable.

WHAT/Purpose:

I would like to make a friend.

HOW: *Pick the one based on the person's relationship ranking.*

WHO: High/Medium Relationship Ranking

This would be an unusual ranking for this situation. It might only arise if you were trying to improve your relationship ranking with a family member.

Example:

"You know, I care about you. I wish we knew each other better. Would you like to talk sometime?"

WHO: Low Relationship Ranking

1. Introduce yourself.
2. State how you know them.
3. Ask the person his or her name.
4. State something that you like about them or what they are doing.

Example:

"Hi, my name is Eli. I know you from class. What is your name?

(Pause for a response).

"I really liked your presentation in class the other day."

(Continue the conversation if the person shows they are interested. Ask questions that show you are interested in them.)

(At some point say…)

"We seem to have a lot of things in common. It might be fun to talk sometime."

WHO: No Relationship Ranking

Example:

"Excuse me. I noticed that we might have _____ *in common. What is your name?"*

(State your name and offer a handshake).

(Continue the conversation if the person shows they are interested. Ask questions that show you are interested in them.)

In an Emergency

Examples:

"I know I don't know you but I might be able to help you. Do you mind if I help out?"

OR

"I know we don't know each other, but I really need help. Can you help me?"

WHAT/Purpose:

Someone asked me to go out alone with them and I WANT to go.

Special Note: Read the Special Section: Falling in Love.

The most important thing that I can say here is to be sure that the person you want to go out with alone is someone with a high or medium relationship ranking. It is imperative that the person you go with is someone that you can trust and that you have known long enough to have confidence that you will be safe! Know how you will be traveling. Will you be safe? As far as your responsibilities, be sure you have taken care of the responsibilities you have to others prior to going. Do you have any pets that need to be fed or people you have already made promises to meet? In other words, what needs to be done before you leave? It's also a good idea to tell someone you trust where you will be going and when to expect you back so that they could find you, if needed.

HOW: *Pick the one based on the person's relationship ranking.*

Basic approach for all examples:

1. Say what you'd like to do.
2. Thank the person.
3. Ask for details: the when, where, how.

4. Be sure to tell someone you trust where you are going and when to expect you back.

WHO: High/Medium Relationship Ranking

Example:

"That sounds great, Julie. Thanks for inviting me. So when do you want to get together? Do you want to meet there or do you want to go together?"

WHO: Low/No Relationship Ranking

Two words: Don't go! OR, invite an additional friend to go with you so that you have a safety net in case things go wrong. Call a loved one with whom you have a high relationship ranking and be sure to let them know where you are going and when you're expected back. Promise to call that person by a certain hour, so that they can find you if you need help. Take a cell phone with you and some money to take a cab home if you are left stranded.

In an Emergency

This situation would be rare but might arise, for example, if there is someone you love who has been hurt and you are offered a ride to the hospital or something like that. Do what you must in an emergency but be sure that the person you travel with has a high or medium relationship ranking, is an officer, EMT, or fireman (who has a badge and preferably a uniform!).

WHAT/Purpose:

Someone asked me to go out alone with them and I DON'T want to go.

Before you say no, be sure that this is not a situation where you should do it to show that you care. For example, if your mom asks you to go to the movies with her and you don't want to go, GO! She has done a lot for you (some of which she did not want to do either). Another example, might be a best friend asking you to go to an event, such as a dance or a family event. It may not be your favorite thing to do but it is like putting money in the bank of friendship. If you do not make an "investment" of time with your family and friends, it can hurt your relationship with them.

If you really don't want to go, though, here is the basic approach for all examples:

1. Thank the person for the offer.
2. Explain without hurting their feelings, why you can't go.

3. (If you are not going because you just don't feel like going, I don't recommend you say that. It is better to make a polite excuse that doesn't reveal your true feelings.)

4. Alternatively, suggest that you go at a different day and time.

HOW: *Pick the one based on the person's relationship ranking.*

WHO: High Relationship Ranking

It is always tough to say no to someone that you know loves you and who you love in return. Or, you may not want to go because you don't like the person enough to go, you have too much work, you are too tired, or you have little to no interest in the activity. Whatever the reason, be sensitive about how you say you don't want to go.

Example:

"Dad, thanks so much for inviting me! I know how much you love the auto show. Would you mind if I passed? I am really tired and I still have a lot of things to get done tonight (or tomorrow or whenever)."

WHO: Medium Relationship Ranking

Example:

"J.C. Thanks for thinking of me. I am pretty swamped with work and school right now. Do you mind if I take a rain check?"

("To take a rain check" is an expression that means "maybe later.")

WHO: Low/No Relationship Ranking

While it is always important to be polite, people with whom you have low to no relationship do not need to know why you can't go except in a very general way.

Example:

"Thank you for the invitation. I will not be able to attend, but thank you for thinking of me."

In an Emergency

In a true emergency, you may really need to do something you may not want to do. If the emergency requires you to go to the hospital in an ambulance or to follow behind an ambulance with a friend to meet an injured or ill person at the hospital, you'll need to go. Just be sure you are going with someone who is an official (fireman, ambulance driver, etc.) or that you ask someone you trust to accompany you.

WHAT/Purpose:

Someone I know is very ill or is dying.

HOW: *Pick the one based on the person's relationship ranking.*

WHO: High Relationship Ranking

Showing our love to someone who is very ill or may be dying can be as difficult as actually coping with someone's death. People who are ill or dying need a lot of our support and help. They may require us to do things that we don't want to do; but it is important that we do them in order to show love and respect.

Most of us don't want to do anything or see anything that is embarrassing or even gross; but, we must be highly aware of verbal and nonverbal cues we send out that might say we do not want to help. You need to be willing to do things to help.

You also need to know how to ask them what they need, or even know what they really need. Regardless of my advice here, it is really important that you get help from a loved one of high or medium relationship ranking to help you know the best thing to do.

The basic approach here in all cases is to ask questions that will be helpful in aiding you to know what to do. Sometimes, people do not want to be a burden on others and they may say that they are fine or that they do not need anything, even when they do. That can be very confusing for someone with Asperger's who can be dependent on people being clear and explicit with them.

Here are some questions that you should ask, as long as the person is well enough to answer you or is not frustrated by you asking too many questions. You will notice that the questions are very specific because often times, people are embarrassed to accept help and they may try to dismiss you. Whatever you do, don't ask them too many questions at one time.

Example questions:

1) *May I get you something to drink or eat?*

2) *Do you need your glasses? (if applicable)*

3) *Do you need an extra pillow or a blanket?*

4) *Would you like a sweater?*

5) *Would you like to watch some television or listen to the radio?*

6) *Would you like me to turn off (or on) the lights?*

7) *Do you need a doctor or a nurse?*

8) *Do you need me to call someone for you?*

9) *Are you due for another dose of medicine? Can I get it for you?*

10) *Can I sit with you for a while and keep you company?*

11) *Would you like me to pray with you?*

You may even consider simply bringing him or her a "creature" comfort (such as a pillow, a blanket, a magazine, a DVD, etc.) or a token of food (ask the person or his or her primary caregiver before doing this). If it is a child, you might bring him or her a simple toy or stuff animal. Check with a family member of this person before bringing flowers because there may be issues with allergies that will cause a problem to the ill or dying person. Whether or not they use the gifts you bring, it will show you care.

If the ill person is someone who lives in your home, your responsibility increases and the questions above should be asked very frequently, as often as every hour or two, unless it would bother the person. It is okay to ask what they would like for you to do. You may also need to take initiative because the ill person may not even know what they need. If you are in doubt of what they need, you can call another family member, call a doctor, or call an ambulance, particularly if he or she is having trouble breathing or is in great pain. Ask permission of the person before doing so, however.

Be sure you are aware of any medicines the person may be taking or any other important health issues that may impact his or her recovery or must be attended to, even if it is not part of the primary illness (for example, if the ill person has the flu, they may still have to take medicine for their heart every day).

If this is not someone who lives in your home, be sure that you check in on the persons who are the primary caregivers of these ill persons. They, too, may be inclined to tell you that they are fine, so ask specific questions here, too:

Example questions of what you might ask a caregiver of a person who is ill:

1) How are you doing?

2) Do you need a hug?

3) Do you want to talk about it?

4) You must be tired. Can I come over to the house and relieve you?

5) You must be hungry. Can I get you anything to eat or bring you a meal?

6) Is there something I can do to help you?

Or, you can simply say,

"I know this is really hard on you. Please take care of yourself."

Finally, make a plan in your schedule to check in regularly with both the ill person and his or her caregiver. During an intense illness, check in every day or every other day. As someone is recovering, follow up each week for a couple of weeks to be sure that the recovery is still steady and that there isn't anything you can do.

WHO: Medium Relationship Ranking

When you are not a member of an immediate family, you will need to make some changes to the helpful and kind acts you can do for someone struggling with a serious illness. Talk with a member of the person's most immediate family member and ask how you can help. You could suggest to them, as examples, some of the things noted in the high relationship ranking, but don't act without permission.

WHO: Low Relationship Ranking

With people you do not know well, there would be no expectation in society for you to do the things mentioned in the high relationship ranking section. In these cases, it is best to send a card or flowers. It would be appropriate to speak with friends or family members of the person and ask if you there is any way you could help, but, typically, you would not be asked to do anything. If this is someone in your school or office, in addition to a card or flowers, a kind word to others who are closer to the person may be appropriate.

WHO: No Relationship Ranking

With people you do not know at all or people who have been ranked by you in this category for reasons of abuse, you would not be expected to do anything. The best advice that can be given, in this situation, would simply require you not to speak ill or make light of the situation with anyone.

In an Emergency

In an emergency, a person who is ill or dying would typically be attended to by emergency personnel. You may be the person asked to call 911, if the situation happens unexpectedly. Ask those helping the ill or dying person if you can help.

Toolkit Worksheet

What are other situations that you have found to be an issue? Name the situation here and determine your plan. Return here later and report what you actually said. (See p. 128 for directions on how to use this worksheet).

WHO: _____Relationship Ranking_____

WHAT (purpose):_____

WHERE: _____

Hidden Rules? If yes, what?_____

_____

HOW (describe below):

What I plan to say (can I use the basic strategy? Y/N):

What I actually said (to be filled in later):

Describe the difference and why (to be filled in later):

SPECIAL SECTION: FALLING IN LOVE

Now, you may be thinking, the last thing you may want is for someone like me to be teaching you anything about falling in love. I can't blame you. Falling in love is kind of personal and is kind of a grown up thing, too. You may not really fall in love until you are fully grown or close to being grown.

What you need to know is that no matter how old you are, falling in love is confusing—for everyone. Everyone wonders things like, "is this real love and will it last?" "What should I do about my feelings?" "Does the person I am in love with love me back?" As you get older, you will also ask questions like, "Is marriage right for me?" "Would I make a good spouse?" "Is the person I love suited for marriage?" "What kind of a marriage do I want?" No one can say that he or she knows with certainty the answers to all of these questions. For this reason I compare love to a tool such as a paintbrush. Love, like a paintbrush, is not precise. It is something you will learn to use little by little. Sometimes it will be messy, other times, you'll make just the right move and the picture will come out looking pretty good!

Many lucky people find long-lasting love the first time; other people try for many years and may not find it or get it right. What you need to know is that there are things you can say or do to protect your heart and to take appropriate chances in order to find the right kind of love. In this section, I will talk about some general knowledge we do have about successful relationships, some things a person with Asperger's may need to be mindful of when considering being in a very serious relationship, and a reminder about what true emotional intimacy is.

There is a lot of research that tells us things about what most successful relationships have. Most, not all, but most people have better luck in relationships where they share a lot in common such as beliefs, backgrounds, and interests. For example, research tells us that people with the similar backgrounds have longer lasting marriages. Other traits that can help with successful marriages are similar faiths, similar ages, and similar education. While people with lots in common sometimes don't make for a good relationship, statistics tells us that they are more successful, more often.

Each of us alone has the power to decide what we want in a mate and what kind of a relationship we want. As a person with Asperger's, you may have one advantage you can use here. You can be very logical: so use it! When looking for a spouse, we should look for someone who we respect, who we can have a deep conversation with; we should look for someone who makes good choices in their own life, and for someone who shares special interests with us. In other words, look for someone who wants the same things out of life as you do. For example, perhaps you do not want to have children or the person you are interested in disagrees with you about something you believe in strongly, such as religion—be very cautious about getting involved with this person. If you are not careful and thoughtful, it could cause you great emotional pain, no matter how attracted to them you are now. This is because core beliefs and traits impact our lives on a daily basis.

For example, if you are a messy person and you marry someone who is very neat, it could create a lot of conflict, every day—to the point of threatening the stability of the relationship. It may not show up early in your relationship because you aren't around each other every day, all day. Whatever you do, I urge you to get to know the person well so that you can find any incompatibility that may exist between you. Even once you visit your love-interest's home, you may be so attracted to him or her and so in love with the idea of being in love that you will ignore the issue. Or, if your loved one lives with someone else who may be caring for the home, you may not see the issue. So, use your intelligence to make good decisions about love. Love doesn't feel logical, but you can use logic when making decisions about love.

Even once you are in a stable relationship, relationships take work; and you have to spend a lot of time to make them work. People with Asperger's do have romantic relationships and successful marriages. What their partners sometimes complain of, though, is that sometimes their feelings are ignored or not recognized. Some partners complain that there is no excitement or newness in the relationship. Others complain that they are not able to enjoy fulfilling physical intimacy.

All of these things are issues you will need to consider for yourself. Are you able to provide your partner all of the things that he or she needs? I am not talking about money or things. I am talking about how much touching, how many words, and what types of actions it will take on your part to show love to your partner every day. It will take lots of conversations throughout the life of your relationship to find out what your partner wants and lots of soul-searching to know if you want to do the work required.

When my stepson Eli was very young, we talked a lot about him needing to do things with others that were not so interesting to him, from time to time, in order to ensure that people would want to do things with him—that it was an important step to making friends). This means that when we have relationships with people, sometimes we have to do things for them that aren't always our favorite thing to do. By doing these things, though, we build trust and show love to each other. In romantic love, it is the same thing. As long as you are never asked to do something that could hurt you or makes you feel bad about yourself, and your partner tries to enjoy those things that make you happy, you should make an effort to do things that bring joy to your partner. If you do not, the relationship may not last very long. Your partner will become frustrated, sad, and even angry. He or she will resent doing all of the kind and loving things he or she does for you. He or she will demand you change and show your love. I have told Eli for years that love is an action, not just a feeling. Over the years, we taught him this by having him take care of himself, of pets, of our household, and of family members. If you can believe it, romantic and marital love is even more work. We must know what our special partner needs to feel special with you.

We also need to talk about the issue of emotional intimacy. We have used the Relationship Ranking Scale a lot in this book, and that scale is a great place to start in knowing how much trust and closeness we can have with someone. What is different when talking about being in love is that when we have romantic feelings for someone, we want to kiss, hug and have physical contact with him or her. We will also want to do things that are best saved for a long-term permanent relationship. Because physical intimacy can lead to pregnancy, disease, and very strong feelings that we sometimes feel like we can't control, it is very important that you, as a person with Asperger's, take extra care with your feelings and know with some sureness that your feelings are returned and valued by the other person. Even when people don't struggle with understanding other people's emotions like you sometimes do, they can easily be convinced that there is something more to a relationship than is actually there and end up doing things and saying things that they later regret.

I don't say these things to scare you away from love. I didn't find my own love until I was nearly 40 years old. I thought I'd never find true love, but I have. And, it has brought me great joy and peace. Perhaps, that is my message to you. You should feel deep, lasting happiness and peace with the person you love. It should not hurt; it should be returned fully by the other person. It should make you feel good about yourself. It should make you feel secure. It should make you feel like you should be a better person. If you don't feel all of these things with the person you are with, you may want to consider if it is the right person for you. It doesn't make him or her or you a bad person. He or she may just not be the right person for you.

Whatever happens, love yourself, too. You cannot find happiness with someone else if you are not happy with yourself. Develop yourself as a person while you wait for true love. Go to college, find interesting hobbies, develop philosophies or religious faith, take care of your body, and make lots of friends. In the end, you will be more interesting to a romantic partner if you are accomplished and confident with these matters!

Julie Hutchins Koch, Ph.D.

IMPORTANT DEFINITIONS

There are some terms you'll need to know when using this book (and for life). Remember that that the terms will not be words that are new to you but rather words whose meaning we'll need to agree on in order to make sure your response is the most appropriate it can be. Goggles are a tool that you put in front of your eyes to protect them while allowing you to still see clearly. Familiarizing yourself with words that have to do with relationships and working with people is important. If you define them a little differently than I do, that's okay. Just use them this way when you use the book so things will be consistent and logical.

Acquaintance: someone you know because you share a situation or brief encounter. Examples of an acquaintance may be the clerk you regularly see at the local grocery store, a classmate with whom you don't spend any one-on-one time, or someone you met briefly at a school dance. Whatever the case, an acquaintance is not someone you would do things socially with. An acquaintance is low on the Relationship Ranking Scale).

Attire: the clothes we wear.

Associate: someone you know because you work with them, whether at work or at school, usually they would be someone you currently spend time with in order to complete a task. Examples of an associate might be a co-worker, a college classmate, a school mate, or a friend from church. Whatever the case, an associate is not someone you would normally do things socially with—unless it is at a party, at the office, school, or church.

Boundaries: the invisible barriers between people. Boundaries can include emotional, social, physical or behavioral boundaries between you and another person. Examples include:

• emotional boundary: feelings between two people that either prevent or encourage them from spending time with each other, touching each other, sharing personal information, etc.

• social boundary: a hidden rule that discourages or encourages us to participate in a social function. For example, at school, you will notice that some people tend to eat with the same people every day. It is not spoken, but, often, others are not really welcome to join.

• physical boundary: the space that a society says we can have between us when speaking or interacting.

• behavioral boundary: the rules that a place might have in place to keep good order, such as a classroom or school, a bank, or a long line.

Boyfriend/Girlfriend: someone with whom you have a verbal agreement which says you regularly date or correspond with each other either in a romantic way. Some agreements between boyfriends and girlfriends say they are exclusive (meaning that you only date or correspond with that one person in a romantic way), or not exclusive (meaning that you agree that you can date other people romantically, too). An important note here is that in order to avoid any misunderstandings, you should discuss with your romantic friend that not only can you call each other a boyfriend or girlfriend but that you are or are not exclusive. I would also recommend that you understand that the most important part of "boyfriend" or "girlfriend" is that you are also real friends. If you base your feelings for your boyfriend or girlfriend based only on sexual or romantic feelings, you may be taken advantage of.

Classmate: see Associate.

Colleagues: see Associate

Culture: the beliefs, customs, art, language, history, attitudes, food preferences, and dress of a group of people.

Customs: these are the spoken and unspoken rules in a society or subculture. Examples of customs may include how a family or group or community celebrates a holiday, how people greet each other, or how people expect each other to behave in certain situations. Be aware that it is okay to ask about what the customs of a family, group or community are. It is recommended that you ask a family member, friend or associate instead of asking an acquaintance or a stranger.

Emergency: an emergency is a situation that must be handled immediately due to the danger it poses to you and/or someone else. It requires your immediate attention. In a serious emergency, you may hear people cry, scream, yell, collapse, or bleed. It is important that you determine very quickly what you should do to help or avoid the emergency. You will need to drop what you are holding and/or stop what you are doing or talking about.

Emotional Intimacy: intimacy is defined as a feeling of closeness between two people. (It can be physical, emotional and or/sexual). Emotional intimacy can be difficult to understand because what makes some people feel close may not make other people feel close. However, generally speaking, feeling emotional intimacy with someone usually includes being able share a secret with someone and know that it will not be repeated to someone else, being able to depend on someone to listen to you share your feelings, or being able to spend extended amounts of time alone with people who make you happy.

Family: While some people think that family is simply defined by biological relationships, such as parent, sibling, cousin, or grandparents, some people may earn a spot in your life as family members. These may include adoptive parents, step-family, long-time family friends, or personal friends whom you've known for many years. The important thing to remember is that all family members still must earn your trust and may not be worthy of your time, attention or respect. For example, be careful when meeting people who are introduced to you as family but that you do not know personally. These new family members must still earn their closeness and trust with you over time.

Fiancé: This is someone with whom you are engaged to be married. As a rule, people who are engaged have had a long-term intimate relationships (and a high ranking on the Relationship Ranking Scale) have verbally agreed to be married on a certain date in the near future, have exchanged a ring indicating their promise to each other, and plans are currently being made to have a legal ceremony of marriage. Sometimes when we have a boyfriend or girlfriend, our feelings lead us to say things that may feel like we're engaged but having a ring, a date and an active plan are the only true indicators that your relationship is heading toward something permanent. My mother used to say that in order to be engaged, you must have a ring and a date!

Friend: the term "friend" is thrown around in our society somewhat loosely. You've probably heard teachers call their students friends, parents refer to their children as friends, or schoolmates refer to you as a friend; however, true friends are people, that through time and experience, have proven themselves to be trustworthy and caring. In the same way that boyfriends and girlfriends have a verbal agreement to be special to each other, true friends agree that they are friends, tell others that they are your friend, spend time with you alone or in small groups, and that we have personal knowledge of and who have personal knowledge of us. Usually friends have spent time at each other's houses and know important information about each other such as full names, addresses, phone numbers, and what they like, or what they like to do. If you feel like you are friends with someone, ask yourself how much time you have spent with them, if you both have each other's contact information, and if they have taken time to know how things are going in your life. A final note about friends and friendship is that it is important for you to take time to invest in your friends. It means asking them questions about their lives, knowing both familiar and intimate details about them, and spending time doing things they like to do (even when it is not your favorite thing to do).

Important vs. Urgent: unlike an emergency, an important or urgent situation may not pose an immediate danger to you or someone else, but it is a situation that must be resolved immediately or as soon as possible. Examples of important vs. urgent include:

- Important situations are a high priority to the people who say they are important. To a person who says something is important, you must understand that either it is important to you, too, or that you must respect that the other person feels it is important and act accordingly. Important situations don't always have to be handled immediately but you should ask key people in the a situation when and how these situations should be handled. Some important situations (that are not urgent) may include setting aside time for family and friends, following a plan to complete a task at work, or paying a non-delinquent bill. Remember that all important situations will eventually become urgent if they are not completed or resolved.

- Urgent matters are those that must be handled immediately or as soon as possible. Urgent situations are not always the most important priority, but because of a circumstance they must be resolved very quickly. Some urgent (but not necessarily important) situations may include turning in a form on time, acknowledging the receipt of a message or filling the gas tank.

- Keep in mind that some situations are both important and urgent (but not emergencies). This combination may include arriving to a job interview on time, going to the doctor to treat a non-life threatening health condition, or spending time with a friend or family member who is in need.

- Emergencies are always both urgent and important. These situations must be given all of your attention. They are usually life-threatening or may cause irreparable harm to someone's life, home, or livelihood. Emergencies are always unexpected.

Handshake: It is important to discuss what a good handshake is. A handshake is a traditional greeting in Western cultures, like the U.S., and many other cultures, too—although not all cultures. It is used to greet strangers and friends alike. A good handshake is almost always offered with the right hand, unless you are the person you are greeting has an impairment making a right-handed handshake difficult or impossible. In those circumstances, you should offer your other hand and modify the grip. A handshake should be firm, meaning your hand should be stiff, NOT soft. You should give a light squeeze but not hard. Practice your handshake; it tells people a lot about you, your confidence and your concern for them. See also the definition of a Warm Handshake.

Hidden Curriculum: Hidden rules. Also see Customs

Norms: see Customs.

Platonic: a platonic relationship is a friendship that is not romantic. As with most friendships, this must sometimes be defined verbally between two people. However, we can use cues from our interactions with people to know if a relationship will only be platonic. Some cues we see in platonic relationships include the absence of touch between the two people and no romantic language (see definition of romantic). Platonic relationships ("just friends") do not involve sexual touching or sexual intercourse of any kind.

Private: private situations or privacy can be defined simply by the number of people with whom we want to share an experience. If we share the experience with only ourselves, it is very private; this may include bathing, dressing or sleeping. If we share an experience with just one other person, it can be private if the interactions include the sharing of secrets or romantic touch; these situations should be shared only with someone whom we have built intimacy and trust. Some private matters can be shared with more than one person but usually would be reserved for family or close friends; these may include health matters, financial matters or school or career matters.

Relationship: A relationship is the emotional closeness, trust or intimacy you feel (or don't feel) with someone. You can be familiar with someone whom you do not feel emotionally close. Being familiar with someone simply means that you know a lot about another person. Having a close relationship with someone likely includes biographical information about his or her life, or it may include knowledge of someone's personal habits, attitudes or beliefs—BUT, this does not mean that you are emotionally close. To learn more about what your relationship with someone else might be, use the section of the book called the Relationship Ranking Scale.

Romantic/Romance: While romance is very hard to define, it is generally thought of as a feeling of intimacy between two people who are attracted to each other emotionally and physically. We can feel emotionally close to someone but not feel physically attracted; this is not romantic. Conversely, we can feel physical attraction for someone with whom we do not have an emotional intimacy with; this is not romantic, either. We must be very careful as we develop and define romantic relationships; most importantly, it is important to remember that true romance must include mutual feelings between two people. In other words, both you and the other person must be able to verbally express your romantic feelings for each other. While it can be embarrassing and scary, it is especially important that we do not assume that someone feels the way we do about them and that we exchange words between each other that tells us clearly that they feel romantically for us and vice versa. Examples of romantic language that may provide clear indicators that someone has good feelings for you are words like, "I like you," "I like spending time with you," "You are important to me," and "I miss you when you're not here." Caution: do not trust the words someone says without appropriate time and actions to indicate that the person means what they say. In other words, read the definition of friend, boyfriend/girlfriend above. Always ask yourself, "How much time you have I spent with them? Do I know this person's contact information? Have they spent time with me recently without expecting romantic language or romantic touch? Do they listen to me? Do they share my feelings?". Remember, romantic language can lead to romantic touch. Except for a handshake or a friendly pat on the back, do not allow someone to touch you unless you have confidence that they are a true friend and that you can trust them.

Situation: Generally speaking, a situation is all of the set of circumstances one person finds themselves in. In this book, a situation can be defined as the collection of all the circumstances that are involved in working with a person. It is the combination of the answers to the questions: who, what, how, and where. We must know all of the answers to these questions in order to understand the whole "situation." Look for these in the Toolkit.

Setting (where): This is the location/place where you are having an interaction with someone. A setting can tell us what society expects that we can say or do in that place. It is the answer to the question "where" and will help you get started with making a plan for communicating with someone effectively.

Spouse (Husband/Wife): This is only someone with whom you are legally married. While this may seem fairly obvious, even people without Asperger's find love so confusing that they treat boyfriends/girlfriends or fiancés as though there is a serious, long-term and legal commitment to each other. Protect your feelings. Don't play "house" with someone who has not made an open commitment to you and with whom you have not made a commitment. I do not say this to pass moral judgment; it is an important for you to remember, as someone who has Asperger's, that you may be vulnerable to misunderstandings about love and commitment.

Street Smarts vs. Book Smarts: Sometimes, I will refer to someone with Asperger's as having amazing "book" smarts. This just means that some of us are wonderful at learning new knowledge and applying it. Most people with Asperger's have an amazing capacity for "book" smarts. Sometimes, though, Asperger's can get in the way of developing "street" smarts or what could also be referred to as practical or common sense. Not having "street" smarts does not mean you are not smart and it doesn't literally refer to city streets. It just means that you will have to take extra steps in life to learn how to understand other people's words, actions and motivations. You can learn street smarts through experience, reflection, and the help of trusted friends and family. I hope this book will help you develop your "street smarts."

Warm Handshake. A warm handshake is a handshake with an added touch to show special love or concern (see Handshake). You might want to use this handshake when you are aware that the person you are greeting is undergoing a hardship or if you are very glad to see this person after some time away or after they have shown special kindness to you. Please be sure you are familiar with the qualities of a good handshake. When offering a warm handshake, you'll shake hands then reach your free hand (usually your left hand) to the elbow or shoulder of the person you are greeting. You can squeeze lightly with the hand. You will want to be shaking the other hand and making the special touch at the same time, so you will want to practice this handshake, too. You would use a warm handshake with a relative or close, personal friend. You wouldn't use it with someone at work or school, unless you had a very special, positive relationship with the person.

ABOUT THE AUTHOR

Julie Hutchins Koch, Ph.D., lives in St. Louis, Missouri with her husband Drew and her step-son, Eli. She has worked in the field of education for over 25 years, including teaching, school administration, curriculum development, training and educational video production. She has experience in all levels from elementary school to graduate school, urban to suburban environments, public to private settings, non-profit to profit organizations, and in state education agencies. She enjoys writing about educational topics in her free time, including fiction and non-fiction.

Julie Hutchins Koch, Ph.D.

Toolkit Worksheet

What are other situations that you have found to be an issue? Name the situation here and determine your plan. Return here later and report what you actually said. (See p. 128 for directions on how to use this worksheet).

WHO: _____**Relationship Ranking**_____

WHAT (purpose):_____

WHERE: _____

  Hidden Rules? If yes, what?_____

_____

HOW (describe below):

What I plan to say (can I use the basic strategy? Y/N):

What I actually said (to be filled in later):

Describe the difference and why (to be filled in later):

Toolkit Worksheet

What are other situations that you have found to be an issue? Name the situation here and determine your plan. Return here later and report what you actually said. (See p. 128 for directions on how to use this worksheet).

WHO: _____**Relationship Ranking**_____

WHAT (purpose):_____

WHERE: _____

Hidden Rules? If yes, what?_____

_____

HOW (describe below):

What I plan to say (can I use the basic strategy? Y/N):

What I actually said (to be filled in later):

Describe the difference and why (to be filled in later):

Toolkit Worksheet

What are other situations that you have found to be an issue? Name the situation here and determine your plan. Return here later and report what you actually said. (See p. 128 for directions on how to use this worksheet).

WHO: _____Relationship Ranking_____

WHAT (purpose):_____

WHERE: _____

    Hidden Rules? If yes, what?_____

_____

HOW (describe below):

What I plan to say (can I use the basic strategy? Y/N):

What I actually said (to be filled in later):

Describe the difference and why (to be filled in later):

Toolkit Worksheet

What are other situations that you have found to be an issue? Name the situation here and determine your plan. Return here later and report what you actually said. (See p. 128 for directions on how to use this worksheet).

WHO: _____**Relationship Ranking**_____

WHAT (purpose):_____

WHERE: _____

    Hidden Rules? If yes, what?_____

_____

HOW (describe below):

What I plan to say (can I use the basic strategy? Y/N):

What I actually said (to be filled in later):

Describe the difference and why (to be filled in later):

Toolkit Worksheet

What are other situations that you have found to be an issue? Name the situation here and determine your plan. Return here later and report what you actually said. (See p. 128 for directions on how to use this worksheet).

WHO: _____ **Relationship Ranking** _____

WHAT (purpose): _____

WHERE: _____

Hidden Rules? If yes, what? _____

_____

HOW (describe below):

What I plan to say (can I use the basic strategy? Y/N):

What I actually said (to be filled in later):

Describe the difference and why (to be filled in later):

Toolkit Worksheet

What are other situations that you have found to be an issue? Name the situation here and determine your plan. Return here later and report what you actually said. (See p. 128 for directions on how to use this worksheet).

WHO: _____**Relationship Ranking**_____

WHAT (purpose):_____

WHERE: _____

    Hidden Rules? If yes, what?_____

_____

HOW (describe below):

What I plan to say (can I use the basic strategy? Y/N):

What I actually said (to be filled in later):

Describe the difference and why (to be filled in later):

Toolkit Worksheet

What are other situations that you have found to be an issue? Name the situation here and determine your plan. Return here later and report what you actually said. (See p. 128 for directions on how to use this worksheet).

WHO: _____Relationship Ranking_____

WHAT (purpose):_____

WHERE: _____

    Hidden Rules? If yes, what?_____

_____

HOW (describe below):

What I plan to say (can I use the basic strategy? Y/N):

What I actually said (to be filled in later):

Describe the difference and why (to be filled in later):

Toolkit Worksheet

What are other situations that you have found to be an issue? Name the situation here and determine your plan. Return here later and report what you actually said. (See p. 128 for directions on how to use this worksheet).

WHO: _____**Relationship Ranking**_____

WHAT (purpose):_____

WHERE: _____

    Hidden Rules? If yes, what?_____

_____

HOW (describe below):

What I plan to say (can I use the basic strategy? Y/N):

What I actually said (to be filled in later):

Describe the difference and why (to be filled in later):

Toolkit Worksheet

What are other situations that you have found to be an
issue? Name the situation here and determine your plan.
Return here later and report what you actually said. (See p.
128 for directions on how to use this worksheet).

WHO: _____**Relationship Ranking**_____

WHAT (purpose):_____

WHERE: _____

    Hidden Rules? If yes, what?_____

_____

    HOW (describe below):

What I plan to say (can I use the basic strategy? Y/N):

What I actually said (to be filled in later):

Describe the difference and why (to be filled in later):

Toolkit Worksheet

What are other situations that you have found to be an issue? Name the situation here and determine your plan. Return here later and report what you actually said. (See p. 128 for directions on how to use this worksheet).

WHO: _____ **Relationship Ranking** _____

WHAT (purpose): _____

WHERE: _____

Hidden Rules? If yes, what? _____

_____

HOW (describe below):

What I plan to say (can I use the basic strategy? Y/N):

What I actually said (to be filled in later):

Describe the difference and why (to be filled in later):

DIRECTORY OF SITUATIONS

This is a quick reference guide to the common situations you might encounter. Remember, if you can't find your situation, it may be in the Anywhere and Other General Settings Section, or in another section. Don't worry if your situation is not here. You can use the Toolkit Worksheet to make your own solution.

General Settings/Anywhere

Julie Hutchins Koch, Ph.D.

CPSIA information can be obtained at www.ICGtesting.com
Printed in the USA
LVOW04s1522170415

435049LV00016B/986/P